SPIRIT GUIDES ON SPEED DIAL

A PRAGMATIC APPROACH TO GETTING WHAT YOU WANT

Jules Apollo

UTOPIAN
FOREST

Published 2024 by Utopian Forest, an imprint of Jules Apollo LLC
Printed in the United States of America

ISBN: 979-8-9891599-0-1 (paperback)
ISBN: 979-8-9891599-1-8 (e-book)
ISBN: 979-8-9891599-2-5(audiobook)

Interior design by Choi Messer
Cover design by 100Covers

Although the author has made every effort to ensure that the information in this book was correct at press time, the author does not assume and hereby disclaims any liability to any party for any loss, damage, or disruption caused by errors or omissions, whether such errors or omissions result from negligence, accident, or any other cause.

The resources in this book are provided for informational purposes only and should not be used to replace the specialized training and professional judgment of a health care or mental health care professional. The author of this book does not dispense medical advice or prescribe the use of any technique as a form of treatment for physical or medical problems without the advice of a physician, either directly or indirectly. The author's intent is only to offer information of a general nature to help you in your quest for emotional and spiritual well-being. In the event that you use any of the information in this book for yourself, the author and publisher assume no responsibility for your actions.
https://julesapollo.com

In memory of my brother Mark.
And to my three sons. Love you more than sunshine.

CONTENTS

CHAPTER 1
START WHERE YOU ARE

It's the fall of 1986. I'm sitting in the chipped old bathtub of my apartment near the University of Minnesota's St. Paul campus, where I've just started graduate school after two years of planting trees at the edge of the Sahel desert in Niger, West Africa, with the Peace Corps. I'm trying to find a way to quiet all the voices in my head telling me that I suck so I can have a few minutes of calm, and I've read that sitting in warm water can help.

After quite a bit of work over six months, I am now able to spend a few minutes at a time in quiet meditation. And today, I start noticing white blobs around me when I close my eyes. I'm just curious about these, as they don't feel bad. In fact, they feel great. There's so much gentle love flowing from them.

From that day on, each time I meditated, the blobs were there. And over a few months, the blobs got closer and more defined (but still indistinct figures; I didn't see clear faces). They were some sort of beings of light, as they only felt good. What could they be?

This was before the internet, so the only books I'd been able to find on meditation were dense tomes about Tibetan monks. The only ones that mentioned spirit guides were in the small occult sections of some bookstores, and they didn't give clear steps on how to work with guides, how to start communicating with them, or what it meant if they just started showing up. Were there established spiritual protocols I was supposed to adhere to? It felt strange, like I was invited to a fancy banquet and didn't know how to use all the silverware.

I bought and checked out books from the library on Tibetan Buddhism, Hinduism, Islam, and Christianity, searching for details on anyone who shared visions, such as Hildegard of Bingen, and anything I could find on angels. As far as I could tell, angels were the only type of being of light mentioned in almost every religion.

This went on for a year, me researching and the shapes moving closer, feeling wonderful. As they became more defined, I seemed to see wings. Finally, I asked if they were angels. They got brighter when I asked this, and I felt a huge wave of love surrounding me. I felt energy move up my spine, a kind of click-in-place sensation I've come to know as truth moving through me.

Why were they hanging around me? What did they want? I pulled out of the meditation because it made me so uncomfortable: I thought I must be making it up. But regardless, if they got too close, they'd see I wasn't worth talking to. I had no experience with angels, let alone the belief there was any possible way they'd find me worthy enough to spend time with. I grew up going to a strict Missouri Synod Lutheran church in Iowa, where angels were never mentioned; it was mostly "ask for forgiveness and get back to work."

My need to quiet my inner voices was too strong for me to stop trying to find some peace of mind, though, and over time I became more comfortable around the angels. They showed up in different sizes, all of them exuding peace and love, hovering around me without asking me to do anything.

So, over the next few years, I played with the angels without telling anyone and simply enjoyed their presence. Sometimes I heard the singing of angelic choirs, which was luscious, and sometimes they shared messages of love and support. They didn't seem to want anything.

I looked for books about angels to see if I could figure out whether their different sizes might indicate that they were different kinds of angels, and what those different kinds might be. Some books I found contained representations and lists of the supposed different types of angels and their roles and hierarchies. It took many more months for me to figure out that the tall angels who exuded the brightest light might be archangels.

When I asked if they were indeed archangels and got the same energy hit that felt like a yes, I instantly pulled out of the meditation and didn't go back for a while. There was no reason archangels would want to hang out with me. I was mentally messed up, with lots of voices in my head, and had (still have) a terrible temper. With my low self-esteem, there was no way I could accept archangels showing up to be with me.

But, oh, the love that poured from them! Shutting them out was like asking myself not to butter and shove freshly baked bread into my mouth. I craved the love and acceptance that is always part of their light, that just beams from them. Who doesn't want that? There is so much exuberant joy in their energy; it's not just a still and silent love. So, over time, I got comfortable with them being around.

And my work on feeling worthy of that love began.

It's so difficult for us to feel we are worthy of spirit guidance of any kind, let alone the joyful love we experience when we do tap into it. I see this with students and clients all the time. But what I know from my experience working with people for more than thirty-five years is that we all have a bunch of guides around us all the time. And they're already working with us and want to help, so we might as well lean into that.

What I share in this book comes from decades of learning to work with the different guides who showed up when I quieted my mind, and how I came to see them as my spiritual family. I hope that what I share can bring you some of their peace and comfort as well.

My intention with this book is to give you the tools you need, including proven scripts and tips, to work with your spirit guides starting right where you are today. This process doesn't require you to have an existing spiritual or meditation practice—it doesn't even require quiet, sitting meditation. I can't do that—my brain just doesn't shut up—so I developed other ways to work with my guides. We all have access to inner wisdom from our soul and guides. There are no tests to pass and no gatekeepers to the wisdom and love they share.

You may have sensed your spirit guides before, and worked with them a bit, but haven't created a sustainable practice that works for you: this book is for you, too. It's filled with pragmatic approaches to creating a practice that slips right into your life.

The suggestions I offer aren't tied to any religion or specific belief system and can fit into any practices you already have.

It's about what feels best for you, and all the steps and scripts can be altered.

BUSTING MYTHS

BEFORE YOU START, I WANT to point out some myths about working with spirit guides. My approach is different from what you may imagine is required to receive guidance, and it has worked for my students and private clients as well.

- It doesn't require a quiet space. You can ask your guides for help under your breath even when there is noise and chaos all around you. We learn the practices best in a private place, but that's not a requirement. In fact, times of chaos or stress are the best times to reach out for help, and we're seldom in a quiet space when those are happening. The guides are with you. They'll hear you.
- You don't need big chunks of uninterrupted time. That's unrealistic for most of us. I developed the techniques I share as a single parent with limited time and energy to focus on a lengthy, undisturbed practice.
- You don't need to have a spiritual practice, reach some level of "goodness" or purity of thought, or be forgiven for anything before you can work with your guides. You are good enough just as you are, no matter what you have or haven't done, and you are worthy of all the love and support they are lined up and ready to give you.
- You don't need to know the names of your guides or who they are to start working with them. Getting stuck on

specifics keeps you in your mind instead of your heart, which is where you can best sense guidance.

- You don't need to see, feel, or hear your guides—ever—to work with them. This is part of what makes your life magical; it happens when you ask for help with the assumption that help is coming. You just need to pay attention and notice what happens.
- No special equipment is needed, no singing bowls, incense, meditation pillows, or special loungewear. The guides don't care, they just want to help.

We look to spirit guides to help us by providing answers to our questions, but what has surprised me most about working with guides is how much love they bring. Waves of it, always flowing to us. It's like standing in front of the sun with the heat and light loving, healing, informing, and empowering us all at once. It's amazing and it's always there. The most common message the guides give—at the end of every meditation, every podcast, every session with clients, and every class I teach—is *how deeply loved we are*. The archangels phrase it like this sometimes: *What beauty be this love we have for you.*

Did all of this just blow up your ideas about working with spirit guides? Let's take a few minutes to sit with these statements. I'm sure you have some of these beliefs; I had all of them at one point or another. The ideas that I am worthy of guidance, that I can work with my guides even with all the mistakes I've made, and especially that I am being bathed in love are the ones I've struggled most to accept.

I didn't even realize that self-worth was at the base of so many of my struggles until probably a decade after my guides started showing up, because I didn't yet realize how little I valued myself. I couldn't separate my inner critics from who I was as a person, free of those constraints. But the guides frequently share that we are all divine, that we come from divinity and are created with that energy. They say, repeating it like a mantra: *You are divine, you are holy, you are needed, you are seen.*

If you back away from that text, if you can't yet accept that, it's all good. One of the best benefits of hanging out with your guides, even if you don't sense them around, is that their energy entrains yours, making it easier for you to see yourself as they already see you and the truth of the beauty within you.

If you can give me the benefit of the doubt, accept that the above statements about working with your guides are correct, and are willing to try out the new approaches proposed in this book, you will find that you can easily work with your spirit guides using the processes, tools, and scripts I've provided.

Where did these beliefs about working with spirit guides come from? It used to be that only people trained in meditating for long periods of time (like monks) or people with particular practices (like mystics) could work with guides. You needed a special practice or path and years to develop it, so it was only for people with lots of free time and/or money to pay somebody to teach them.

Forget all that! None of it applies anymore. And it keeps us from tapping into the wisdom that is literally standing right next to us, trying to get our attention.

Look—the planet is messed up. A lot of people are suffering. The world needs all the compassion, wisdom, peace, and power you can bring to the table. These techniques are designed to help bring out the best in you, so let's dive in.

Working with your guides can be an ongoing, rambling conversation, just like you'd have with an old friend—times of comfortable silence, knowing they are there, interspersed with comments and requests. You can get to that point using what I share in this book.

WHY THESE PRACTICES WORK

I UNDERSTAND BEING BUSY: I had three sons under the age of six when I got divorced and no child support or time off from having them with me. I developed practices that didn't require a lot of time or money since I didn't have much of either one.

I don't like to waste my time, so something must help me, or I won't do it. I'm also a scientist, used to testing to see what works and adjusting as needed. How does this relate to what you'll see in this book? These techniques have been tested and revised for efficiency and effectiveness over my several decades of working with hundreds of people.

- They will fit into your life, no matter how much you have going on. They have the single mom seal of approval.
- I'm not going to blather on. This book is lean for a reason. The point is for you to get answers you can trust using steps that fit into your life.
- I know where I (and others) got stuck in the process, so this book offers ways around those pitfalls, too.
- I've taught these techniques to many others, and the steps have worked for them.
- You can discard what doesn't work and revise everything to fit into your life.

YOUR SPIRIT GUIDES ARE ALREADY WORKING WITH YOU

You HAVE MANY GUIDES, ALL of them ready and willing to help you. And in subtle ways, they already have been. We'll look at how you're already getting guidance (even though you may not have realized it was happening) and build upon that using your intention, imagination, and energy to create a practice that's grounded and clear so you can trust the guidance you're receiving.

Through the steps in this book, you'll learn:

- How guidance comes (and how you're already perceiving it in subtle ways)
- Tools to use (you probably already have everything you need)
- How to set up a practice that allows you to trust what you're sensing
- The types of guides that might be helping you
- How to ask for help and understand it when it comes
- How to ask for help in times of trauma
- How you might get stuck and how to address it
- How to work with your guides to go after your dreams
- How to work with your guides to reach your goals
- How to pull it all together into a sustainable practice that fits into your life.

I'll share scripts and tips to help with each step, along with wisdom from my guides to support you. By the end of this book, you'll have the tools you need to get results and trust the guidance you're getting.

MY SPIRIT GUIDES HELPED WRITE THIS BOOK

I WORKED WITH MY SPIRIT guides to get their input as I wrote this book, and they've shared many messages of support for your process as you learn to work with them. You'll find these comments throughout the book, in italics, under the heading "From the Guides." The guides I work with, whom I consider my family, come from all the categories shared in Chapter 3; you have a whole range of helpers waiting to work with you as well.

When I teach this process as a course, my guides share meditations and energies to create a container of light that helps my students understand and feel the presence of their own guides. The words they share here are intended to provide a similar context for you.

Working with my guides has literally saved my life, as I used to feel that I'd made so many mistakes I might as well end it all. And aside from giving my sons squishy hugs, it has brought me the greatest peace and joy of my life. I hope you can find that ease and peace in these pages.

I've used a question-and-answer approach with my guides to provide concrete answers to questions you might have as we go. Here are a couple.

Why are you coming forth to help write this book?

Many people want the support we are right here ready to share. There are a lot of misconceptions about guides: who we are, how we can help, how to get help, how complicated it needs to be. It can be as straightforward as talking to a friend over a cup of coffee. That's what we hope to bring through this book: easy answers, clarity, and comfort when you need it most.

What do you want most for people to get out of the book?

We are right next to you, and our role in your life—and on this planet now—is to help you release tension so you can share your love, gifts, joy, and creativity. They're all needed now.

Our intention is for this book to support the creation of a safe and sacred space, imbued with love and the highest divine light, that cocoons you in support and guidance so you can embody and complete your divine missions and creative expressions with ease, grace, flow, and joy.

I'll end with this short note from Archangel Gabriel, one of my favorite messages ever.

We walk with you and beside you, sit on your bed and help you put on your shoes, sit next to you in the car as you drive to work, and watch movies with you as you eat popcorn. There is no time in your day when you are not in the company of angels. We are beside you in all aspects of life, so that if or when you need our assistance or guidance, we are ready, attendant, and respectful of your choices. Call on us—we are already here.

QUICK CHECK-IN: WHERE YOU ARE RIGHT NOW

SINCE WE'RE STARTING WHERE YOU are now, let's figure out where that is. Here's a brief list of three questions for you to answer to see how you're feeling about working with your guides. It's important to note that this is just to gauge how you feel right now, not to judge yourself or the process. We'll check in again in the middle and at the end of the book to see how things have improved and demonstrate your progress.

Using a range of one to five, with one being the lowest and five being the highest, answer these questions:

- Do you know how to work with your guides?
- Do you know what guidance looks like and how to tell if you're getting it?
- Do you feel confident that you can tell the difference between guidance and just making something up?

Make a quick note of your number for each question to compare with your middle and final results.

Another way you'll measure your progress is by creating a clear image of yourself and how you'll feel once you're able to work with your guides and trust the answers you're getting. Let's imagine this future vision of you: calm, confident, clear, and creating what you want. This is an image I'll remind you of as we move through the book together, so take five minutes and give yourself the time to truly see, hear, feel, and imagine this as real.

It's helpful to have a vision of where you want to get to, and who you'll be once you're there, to drive toward. How do you feel, how does your day go when you're able to work with your guides? How does it feel to know you have support all around you? What happens when you're clear on what to do next to get what you want? How does feeling calm change your days?

I use this approach a lot to try on the feeling, energy, and identity of what I want to achieve. While writing this book, for example, I tried on the identity of a beloved, bestselling author. If I knew that my words were printed and enjoyed and that people shared them, how would I approach my writing each day? Would I be happier? Would I spend more time in the garden relaxing and less time worried about whether I really could express what I want in a way that helps people?

This approach can work if you're focused on a health issue or a financial concern. I also used it when I was looking for a house in a hot market and worried about finding something I could afford that wouldn't be snatched up by other buyers. As I write this, I'm sitting in the kitchen of the house I imagined— not every detail, but the way it feels, how we live in it, its beauty and sense of peace. Focus on the feeling of having and being what you want and ask the guides to help you with the how, when, and where of it.

Make some brief notes on your vision now. You can update it as you go through the book, but having an idea of where you want to be and how you'll know when you get there gives you energy and momentum. You may want to get a notebook specifically for working through the book, or you can use the workbook I created, *Spirit Guides on Speed Dial Workbook*, which is available wherever this book was purchased. It includes exercises, journal prompts, check-ins, and scripts to support your progress.

GETTING GUIDANCE

NOTICING AND RELEASING YOUR OLD assumptions and rigid ideas about whether you can do this and how it should work will propel you forward. We'll look at your assumptions, and some of the ways you might block your understanding of the guidance you receive, as we go through the steps of learning to work with your guides.

I want to be clear: This isn't a one-and-done thing. It takes time, energy, intention, and focus to create a relationship with your guides that allows you to ask for and receive guidance, but this is the same with any deep friendship or relationship. How quickly this develops depends on your efforts to reach out to them and pay attention to what comes after that. But you already initiated the relationship by picking this book, so they know you're interested in working with them, and you can begin to deepen the relationship starting with the details shared in Chapter 2.

In fact, you can do it right now by saying, "Hi, spirit guides of highest light, I'm looking forward to working with you. Thanks in advance for the help." They will come closer with hugs and love and help you in every step you take while reading or listening to this book. It's a wondrous thing to feel deeply supported and loved, which is what you are; this book will show you that.

Why did I use the phrase "guides of highest light"? We'll go over that in detail in Chapter 3, but for now, just know it's to make sure you call in guidance that's for your highest good.

It's important to remember that guidance is subtle; you have to pay attention, especially at the beginning. Your body is one of your greatest aids in noticing guidance because a lot of it comes through physical sensations. The guides will use any method they can to get your attention, even license plates or billboards. Here's a short list of ways guidance comes for me and my students and might show up for you:

- Through physical sensations like goose bumps, pressure in your shoulder blades, or warmth in your heart
- A song or dream repeating, providing the answer to a question
- A feeling of optimism, joy, or love washing over you for no apparent reason
- Via external messages, like hearing answers you're seeking in others' conversations, or seeing objects (such as billboards or license plates) that relate to a question or concern you have.

Chapter 3 includes many more examples of how you might receive guidance. All these ways they try to help! Paying attention, so you note the guidance you're receiving, is a playful game and makes life feel magical; it's another layer of reality you weren't aware of before.

Everyone has spirit guides around them. We just need to reach out for their help. Why do we have to reach out? They have assignments to help us out (yes, you have a guardian angel and many other guides with specific skills and expertise), but we must ask as part of our free will. They can and will nudge us as noted above, but we need to show them we're ready for a partnership, a friendship, for them to come in more actively. Not to worry, we'll go over how to start communicating with them in the next two chapters.

HOW THIS BOOK IS ORGANIZED

WE'LL START WITH HOW GUIDANCE comes (and how you're already perceiving it in subtle ways), how to set up a practice where you can trust what you're sensing, types of guides, how to ask for help, and how to work with your guides to reach your dreams and goals. Then we'll pull it all together into a sustainable practice that fits into your life—all with quick tips and scripts along the way so you can start working with your guides from this first chapter.

Knowing you can trust your guides is key to getting great guidance. Giving your trust to just any guide isn't the best way to get started, though. You want quality guidance that's for your highest good. Just because Jimmy Joe's uncle recently passed over and isn't in a body anymore doesn't mean he has wisdom to share. I'll give you simple scripts and practices to create a container of energy surrounding you, a safe space, so you're only getting solid guidance of high energy and love. Although some people have a particular connection and expertise working with the dead, it's not something I'll be teaching in this book, as it may bring you information that isn't for your highest good.

At the beginning of each chapter, I share a related story for reference and to show that you can find a way out of whatever you're experiencing based on the tips and scripts I share on the topic.

As I progressed through my spiritual journey, in addition to dealing with external situations and ways I was holding myself back, I learned how to feel more peaceful and joyful. A major benefit of working with your guides is feeling more ease and joy, and we cover aspects of that throughout the book as well.

So you can get some quick wins, I've included brief exercises throughout the book—small steps you can take as you read—under the heading "Try This." For now, I know you might simply be wondering if you can do this. Chapter 2 goes into the questions I had when I started, and the questions students and clients have shared, so you can see that this will be easier than you think and that you already have lots of support at hand.

By the end of this book, you'll have all the tools you need to work with your spirit guides and trust their guidance. We'll look at the tools and basic framework for communicating with them in Chapter 2.

CHAPTER 2
TOOLS YOU'LL USE

NOTHING FANCY NEEDED HERE, THE only physical tools you'll use are:

- A pen and notebook, or
- A place to take notes or record thoughts in your phone or computer, or
- A pen and the *Spirit Guides on Speed Dial Workbook* I created to go along with this book.

That's pretty much it. We'll discuss using your intention, imagination, and energy later in this chapter, but you already have those.

Though you don't need a lot of tools to get started, it's usual to have questions about how all this works. The next section addresses some of the questions you might have.

Q&A WITH MY GUIDES

I came up with a list of questions that clients and students have asked me about working with guides. I had a lot of these questions and concerns when I started as well. I used the list to help me write this book; I also asked my guides to respond to these specific questions and comments. Their brief responses follow the questions.

> **How do I trust what I've been sensing? How do I know that what I'm sensing is good for me?**

One key is to trust your body, the way your body feels, and what your intuition tells you about what you're doing. Knots of dread in your stomach or a fear response are good indicators that you might want to step back and move a bit more slowly. For many people, goose bumps are an indication that we are right next to you, giving our version of a hug. Setting the intention that you are safe and can trust what you sense is powerful. Learning to trust is also learning to notice just what you are sensing in more detail. Greater focus on, and awareness of that, is part of this journey.

Knowing that it's good for you very much depends on how you frame and approach working with us. While any lesson can provide some learning, the intent is to focus only on working with guides who have your highest good in mind. Those of us on the list provided (in the next chapter) fall within that group. Working with souls that have recently passed out of their human bodies and who are still transitioning into their next state of light can be problematic until you are anchored and cocooned in love, so we gently advise against that at the beginning; this is the reason for the specific phrasing and steps suggested here.

> **What if I don't see, hear, or sense anything? Do I need to be visual or good at meditating to do this? I can't meditate, I don't think this is going to work.**

You probably won't sense anything for a while, and at the beginning, you reach out because you need help or because this interaction and support is something you've been craving. So it can feel like talking in an echo chamber at first. Believing it could happen, that you could have our support even if it's not evident the minute you start, is, in some ways, having faith in yourself: Are you worth the love and comfort of angels? Yes, you are, you definitely are. We intended for the words and even the cover of this book to be infused with our love, and for the experience of reading it and committing to trying the process, to be met with a wave of love and comfort.

These practices don't require the ability to sit and do quiet meditation. If you're comfortable with that approach to quieting your mind, it can be part of your practice with your guides. But it's not necessary. The visualizations included here are similar to the way your mind works when someone tells you a story, or when you read a book and imagine the scenes and what things look like. Nothing difficult. And if visual cues don't work for you, there are many other ways for us to reach out and help you.

You are so deeply loved, so supported, so held, so treasured. We as guides in general—(this is our job, after all) and the specific guides who have chosen to support you in this life—can't wait to share more support with you. Not to tell you what to do, but to answer the questions you ask us and share how we see you: capable of so much great shining! We will help you, just keep trying.

How long does it take to start working? How long do I try before I know if it will work?

That depends in part on how focused you are on perceiving the guidance you're already getting. Reread the answer above and keep asking for help. It is subtle for a reason. We are aware that the power of our love and light could easily knock you over, like an exuberant dog with a toddler, so we hold back and gently nudge and hug you instead.

What kind of questions can I ask? Can I get guidance on anything?

You can ask anything. We provide guidance that supports you and your expansion into the fullness of light that you are. That may seem like a mushy response, but we won't provide guidance if you want to tell someone else what to do. We may also guide you to see what you can change within yourself to support what you truly want (freedom, creative expression, love, comfort, self-confidence, financial security).

Where is the guidance coming from? How do I know that what I'm sensing is valuable and good for me?

From love. It may seem trite and glib to keep mentioning love, but we have so much of it for you. The wisdom we share and the help we give, even if it's just helping you find your keys or a parking space, come from love. We are just gushing with it, full of it, for you. (We also have a great sense of humor and love to laugh.) We know this talk of so much love can make you uncomfortable sometimes, but it is our truth and so we share it.

How do I know I'm not just making this up?

Guidance is always gentle and loving (unless you're about to have a car crash; then we'll jump with greater strength). This is part of how you differentiate our voices from your inner ones: we are never critical or harsh. There is love and support behind all our words that pop into your head and every message we send through external things like books and billboards. Can you sense that love? Doing so is part of learning to communicate with us, and a great benefit of creating a practice to get guidance. From us, there is always love and support. You are not generally so kind to yourself. There is also power, strength, and integrity behind our guidance. It's not blindly complimentary or without merit. If this is a concern, then ask for clarity and support to perceive the difference.

Is it okay to do this if I'm practicing a religion? Does this interfere or conflict with any of that?

This is just a practice of quieting your mind and paying attention. It should not interfere with any of your other practices. If it helps, you can approach this as prayer. Or you can set the intention that the guidance coming forward and the guides you work with are in line with the teachings of your faith. Many of the guides listed (in the next chapter) are part of major religions. Angels are mentioned in many religious texts, for instance.

I'm worried that I just don't have the ability to do this. What if I can never shut my brain up enough to focus on receiving guidance?

Learning to quiet your mind is a huge benefit of these practices, but it can be a great struggle. Asking for support as you learn how to do this, even if you aren't perceiving direct guidance, is very helpful and can help build your trust in the process as incremental improvements happen.

> **I'm worried that I don't have enough time to do this every day with everything else going on. I've never done anything like this, and it seems like it takes years to learn how to do it.**

These practices were developed to fit into your day, even if you feel like you have no time at all. And once you start using them, you'll notice that some of the stresses in your life and on your time ease up or that you find ways around them. As described earlier, they were developed to fit into your life as it is now and don't require a lot of time, money, or space for you to get engagement and support.

> **I'm worried that I don't have any inner wisdom.**

We are so grateful this worry has come forward, for now, we can address it! Know this: to be embodied as a human in this time of great strife and change on the planet is to be a warrior of the light, here for the purpose of sharing your love and gifts and shining your light. Of course, this is a powerful statement, and you might reject it out of hand if you are worried that you don't possess inner wisdom, but we plant the seed now so these words can wiggle their way into your heart. You are worthy of our guidance and support. You have wisdom that can help others, in great part due to the suffering you have experienced and issues you have overcome in your life. Yes, there are others who have suffered more; we are not negating that. But the lessons you've learned, the path you've walked to get to the point where you are reading our words right now—there is wisdom there.

We see it and can share it with you. Include this in your requests for guidance, and we can provide specific details on your wisdom so you can continue gaining more of it and sharing it in this life.

> **I'm worried people will think I'm crazy for making decisions based on what I hear in my head and call guidance.**

Then keep it private. There is no harm in exploring different perspectives and options for pursuing your dreams or dealing with personal issues. This is an internal process, and you can request guidance and pay attention to your body and what you're perceiving around you in response to that request in silence while you are cooking, folding laundry, or commuting to work. You deserve to feel comfortable with the decisions you make about your life, and if reaching out to us for support is part of that comfort, so be it. We are here.

Do you recognize any of these concerns? I've had them all at some point; it took a long time for me to learn to trust that I could understand the guidance, and even longer to feel that I was worth being guided. It's my hope that this book will help you quickly overcome these concerns. If you have more questions, write them down now and see if they are answered in the next few chapters. If not, you can ask your guides to help you with them when you get started.

HOW YOU'LL USE THE TOOLS

As you go through your day, you'll want to take note of the ideas, inspiration, and answers that pop into your head in response to communication with your guides, and you can approach this in whatever way works best for you. Detailed journaling isn't required, but perhaps it's something you enjoy doing (I do). I keep a journal near me in bed, as I often wake up remembering details of dreams that I want to record, or ideas for a novel that occur to me while I'm reading before sleep. You can also record notes to yourself and listen to or transcribe them.

Throughout this book, I provide you with scripts you can use (and revise as feels best) to reach out to your guides. You'll have a process to use for working with them that you'll outline. You might keep this outline on your phone. Using your phone to remind yourself of steps, to take notes on what you're sensing, or to store scripts is handy if you like walking meditations or get inspiration while doing physical work. Doing the dishes can be a spiritual experience if you get clarity or comfort while doing it. I seem to get a lot of answers doing laundry.

If you like to take notes on paper, you can use a spiral notebook like kids use for school; a notebook like a Moleskine; a lined, grid-dot, or blank one—whatever you like. Some notebooks have multiple types of pages you can play with to see what works for you. I used to load up on spiral notebooks when they were on back-to-school sales. Now I usually use an unlined Moleskine with a soft cover. I use a college-ruled notebook when I'm working on a book because for some reason, it's easier for me to organize notes that way. Do you currently have a journaling practice? If so, you can use the same notebook. Or you can get another one that is specific to this work.

Some people keep a very small (2" x 3" or 3" x 4") notebook in their pocket or bag so they can make quick notes throughout the day, wherever they are. No matter how busy you are, you can find ways to fit this into your day—even a few minutes of quiet while you're waiting for your kids (or your parents) to get out of sports events or appointments can get you some answers or inspiration, and the information can be all the sweeter when you get it in small bites throughout your day.

You may already use a notes app on your phone. You can use the same kind of app or program instead of writing in a physical journal.

Do you prefer recording voice notes to writing? Do you get your best inspiration while walking or doing other physical activities, so you record thoughts in the moment? Do the same while you work through this book.

Do you like rituals? Lighting a candle or some incense at the beginning of working with your guides can be a way for your practice to feel sacred and special. Use whatever feels easiest as you're getting your practice started. You can download apps that help you turn off the rest of your digital world and focus for a few minutes. We have so many options.

Based on early reader requests, I've created the *Spirit Guides on Speed Dial Workbook* that you can purchase at bookstores or online to go along with this book. It includes journal prompts, the "Try This" sections, and additional scripts and suggestions for working with your guides.

You can use journals and notes in multiple ways, for example:

- To ask questions you have before you go to bed and then note any dreams you remember when you wake up (it's best to note these before you get out of bed, or you'll forget)
- To set an intention to understand the guidance you get around a question or situation, and then note what you've sensed throughout the day before you go to sleep at night

- To note your experiences once you start using the scripts and tips
- To document your dreams, goals, and progress
- To note any tarot or oracle cards you draw. You can find a list of the tarot and oracle decks I use on my website: https://julesapollo.com/extras.
- To note the outcomes of different rituals you use to connect with your guides. Lighting a candle, meditating in the bathtub, using yoga stretches before you start, and always working with your guides in the same location can help get your mind and body relaxed and quiet so you can perceive subtle sensations more easily.
- To experiment with "automatic" writing. Here's what that means: some people write a question with their normal writing hand, ask the guides for help, and then switch hands and write an answer with their other hand—I've tried this, and it doesn't work for me; I can barely read my regular writing, but some people have a lot of success with it.
- To ask for special support in line with the energies surrounding phases of the moon, solstices, equinoxes, etc., and explore rituals that celebrate these events with your guides.

Don't get caught up in these suggestions now; we'll go over them in more detail in the next few chapters.

MIND AND BODY TOOLS

IN ADDITION TO THE PHYSICAL tools, we'll apply three aspects of your mind and body to help you work with your guides:

- Intention,
- Imagination, and
- Energy, or inspired action.

I provide details below on how each of these applies, and they are referenced throughout the book. Creating a spiritual practice or interacting with your guides is much easier when you use your intention, imagination, and focused energy, but it doesn't need to be strenuous or rigid. I developed most of the practices while I had small kids and little time or energy to focus. You too can set up a practice that works with the time and energy you have available.

I don't keep up practices that don't feel good, so this book is written to help you learn to work with your guides in easy, playful ways.

Although we aren't trained as children to consider these three aspects as part of going after our goals, I consider them special powers that we all have. We might not think that our imagination, for instance, could help us work with our spirit guides or get answers to our problems, but these three aspects are the cornerstones of my spiritual practices. Let's go over them in more detail.

INTENTION

USING YOUR INTENTION FOCUSES YOUR mind and spirit on what you want. For example, in terms of starting to work with your guides, we'll use intention to create a safe space, to decide that you're only interested in guidance and guides of the highest love, and to determine that you will receive guidance that's easy to understand.

Why does this matter? You could leave these intentions out and just start asking for guidance, but don't you want guidance that gives you the best help? That is loving, gentle, and comforting? That gives you confidence in what you're sensing and in any actions you take because of that guidance? Of course you do. I've included a script in Chapter 3 that you can use and revise as you wish to set up this framework from the very beginning. That said, your choice of words isn't as important as your intention to reach out and get help.

I don't think the world is an evil place, but I have encountered negative energies, and they can impact your life in many ways. Most of the time this occurred when I interacted with ghosts, people who had passed but got stuck hanging around here for some reason. That's when I started using my intention to make sure I was only getting the best help I could work with. You won't have to worry about this if you use the scripts and tips shared in the next chapters.

I could go on and on about why intention makes such a difference. To me, it's the spine of this process, the power, the focus, and the drive to get what we're aiming for. The line in the sand, the "You shall not pass!" of Gandalf in *The Lord of the Rings*, fighting back a monster. The point where you say, "That's it, I've had it, I'm never going through this again—I am changing my life *now*."

Having a strong intention to make your life better is what will carry you through implementing the suggestions in this book even on days when you doubt things will ever get better. Your intention is more powerful if you speak it out loud. Our voices carry frequencies of light that send energy into the world. Being intentional with our words (and associated thoughts, of course) anchors our intention on the physical plane and calls in more support for our actions. You can whisper your intention under your breath so it's inaudible to others (or even say the words in your mind with intention), and that works as well. It's the intention that counts.

Once you've established a working relationship with your guides, you can use your intention to work on limiting beliefs and get support to change them. I did this with money, asking for help noticing subconscious patterns and family beliefs that were holding me back, and then asking the guides to help me revise them so my relationship with money supported my goals. I developed mantras that I used (and still use if this comes up) to change the pattern, I worked with my guides to clear old energies from my physical, emotional, mental, and spiritual bodies, and I asked for help to create beliefs and actions to support my financial serenity and sovereignty. This same approach applies to health, work, loving relationships, really anything.

FROM THE GUIDES

Setting your intention calls in the power of your spirit and makes it manifest on the physical plane. If you set the intention to receive clear and constant guidance, this guidance will come forth. People, songs, words, images, overheard conversations, billboards, animals catching your eye: all of these are external ways we might share information with you. This is also part of how your life becomes magical.

TRY THIS

The first intention you can set while you're reading or listening to this book is to intend to work with guides of only of the highest light and love, and for any guidance you receive to be easy to understand and filled with love. Here's a quick script you can say now.

"I intend to be surrounded and supported only by my guides of the highest love and light as I read or listen to this book and work through these processes. I intend to learn to communicate with my guides in a way that is filled with ease, love, and joy. I am grateful for the support. So be it."

Who knows, you might start getting downloads of your guides' messages before you finish this book, so I want to make sure you're ready for it!

Don't worry about memorizing this script or writing it down. It's included in Chapter 3, where you start creating your practice.

IMAGINATION

MY IMAGINATION HAS SAVED MY life many times. I had a rough childhood (it was a different time; hitting kids was okay at home and at school, too). By the time I was seven, I felt like such a burden and a failure that I figured my parents would be better off if I'd never been born. My imagination was where I escaped. Reading has always been my favorite thing for this reason. I never could accept that life is only what we see or experience—there's just too much pain and suffering—so I've always looked for more than just the visible. This means my imagination muscle is strong, and I've leaned into it a lot throughout my life, trying to find a way to make my dreams come true while still dealing with the realities of work and just getting through the day.

You may not think of your imagination as a superpower, but it can be! You'll see me call upon it throughout this book, so I hope you'll give these tips as much of a try as the others.

Using my imagination in my work with my guides has made the biggest difference in how I sense and act upon guidance. Since I struggled to do quiet breathing meditations, I looked for other ways to quiet my mind (I didn't know anything about spirit guides at that point, I was only trying to shut up the nasty voices). I found a few books that talked about visualization and using the imagination to create an inner sanctuary, something I'll share with you in Chapter 11. Using this approach finally gave me some peace of mind, and from there, I started sensing my guides. Creating an inner sanctuary is an optional part of your practice but can be helpful.

I use my imagination every time I work with my guides to focus on my dreams (my mind is very visual, so I create mental movies of what I hope will become real). It's the tool I use to expand my sense of possibility anytime a situation in my life doesn't feel joyful or easy.

Money, health, creativity, available time: all of these can be expanded and anchored in your life when you begin by imagining what would feel wonderful.

FROM THE GUIDES

How do you work with our imaginations as part of giving us guidance?

Many of you had your imagination squashed by your families or the schooling you received. We intend to help you free it.

Your imagination is a way to make your dreams manifest very quickly. And here is why: let's say you want a new home or changes to your home. On the physical plane, you're taught to break your dreams down into doable steps, and there is nothing wrong with that. You might plan to look for the home, then find the home, then find the financing, then move in, and set up your home as you like, all these steps.

When you use your imagination, you see the home as complete. You're in it; you're already filling it with your energy. You're sensing what it's like to cook in your kitchen, seeing your view and the beauty that's all around you, noticing how peaceful it is. Whatever it is you desire in the home is there; whatever it takes to realize that dream is already done. It's the difference between thinking that if you want a tree you need to plant it, water it, and watch it grow and envision the mature tree that shades this home of your dreams. Your imagination can transcend time and space because you are putting your energy into the result that you seek. It is easy, it is powerful, and it can be playful. There is no wrong way to use it.

Einstein said that imagination is more important than knowledge, and he knew what he was doing.

Look at all the ways you can use your imagination as you go through your day. If we start with the assumption that your guides are all around you, you can imagine that help is always at hand when you're looking for a parking space, or when you sit down to create. I use my imagination to see, feel, and hear the details of my dreams coming true, and to experience the presence of my guides talking to me and showing me answers to questions. I'll go into more detail on all of this in the coming chapters, and we dive into getting guidance in the next chapter!

TRY THIS

Let's do an imagination check-in.

- What images or possibilities popped into your head as you read or listened to the message from my guides?
- How do you currently use your imagination to go after what you want?
- Does your imagination kick in when you listen to audio-books or podcasts? Or are you more inspired by images (in decorating, gardening, or cooking magazines, for instance)?
- Is there some time in your past when you stopped using your imagination, maybe due to something someone told you about being an adult or it being a waste of time?

If you were told that imagination is a waste of time or for babies, perhaps you can decide to try the suggestions related to using your imagination in the book. If you know of something that jump-starts your imagination, play with that a bit.

ENERGY

ENERGY RELATES TO YOUR COMMITMENT, focus, and action when you feel nudged to do something. Your commitment is demonstrated by picking up this book and trying out these simple actions. Since guidance comes in myriad ways and can be gentle and still, your focus is on paying attention. Learning to act on what you perceive takes trust in yourself and your guides, and you'll develop that as you work with them.

My students and clients tell me it feels easier to get results when they apply their energy and act upon their urges. One client had just one session with her guides and then used what she felt and heard to act upon urges she'd been having for a while but was afraid to do anything about. She ended up transforming a part of her business to great financial reward. Another client came to me with a financial emergency; her family was facing eviction and she reached out in a panic, even though she thought working with guides was a bit weird (this happens frequently; the approach seems woo-woo until it works, and then it's still weird but okay to use). She ended up calling on Archangel Michael for help and wanted a sign that something was being done, since she was so frightened. She found a feather on her doorstep the next day and feathers in her path for months afterward as the situation resolved and her financial situation stabilized. His guidance is still working for her years later.

Your body can be an important partner in using your energy to receive guidance. I noted in Chapter 1 that your body is on the front line of perceiving guidance, so you might already be aware of how it helps you apply what you're learning in this book. Moving your body can help you receive guidance as well. Here are a couple of ways I use physical movement to support my work with my guides.

Sometimes it helps to grease the wheels a bit and do some movement before meditating to make it easier for your body to adjust to higher frequencies. You could do some easy stretches or yoga for a few minutes, or dance to music that puts you in a contemplative mood or opens your heart. I find that dancing a bit before settling in to reach out for guidance can help me feel grounded, release tension, and get ready for spiritual adventures, all at the same time.

Movement during your meditations or interactions with your guides can support the experience; it helps you go beyond the monkey mind and get inspired. I find that I frequently get great guidance while walking. Some of my students have noticed this happens when they run or work out.

I move if there's something I feel tense about, using the nervous tension to propel the movement and then just quietly waiting for inspiration, as if I'm on the shore of a lake, listening to the waves. When I do this, I set an intention to get clear information and let the guides know I'm tense, so they understand. Swimming, riding a bike, canoeing, or working in the garden are other ways to incorporate movement into meditation.

It may be that you're guided to move during interactions with your guides even if you've been sitting quietly, trying to get answers. Pay attention to your body: it might want to move, dance, or assume a pose. I've had several meditations with my Goddess Council where we were all doing belly dance movements. I find that belly dancing (even stiff, unattractive belly dancing, which is the only kind I can do) helps with creative inspiration. If you've had a past life as a priestess, these types of moves can come quite naturally, since many of the dances came from priestesses' sacred offerings to the goddess and were then absorbed into entertainment. Even if you don't have a Goddess Council—yet—you can invoke a goddess or the Divine Feminine as a muse and inspiration when asking for guidance with a creative project or problem. See Chapter 3 for more details on types of guides, including goddesses.

Your body is the last energetic system to assimilate the energies of your meditation. You are accessing higher frequencies even as you start to ask for guidance. See if you feel like moving after meditation. Get in touch with what your body wants, and you may find that clarity or comfort flows in.

TRY THIS

What movement works for you? How might you incorporate movement into getting messages? What does your body prompt you to do that allows you to receive with ease and joyful grace?

I love to ask a question and then take a walk or clean a closet, letting go of the question. Something frequently pops up in my head as I'm doing something else. Try this to see if it works for you.

Let's move on to Chapter 3, where you'll learn how to start your practice. Don't worry if you're feeling nervous— we'll go through simple steps and scripts together so you feel comfortable and confident that you can do this.

CHAPTER 3
HOW YOU RECEIVE GUIDANCE

IT'S EARLY 1987 AND I'M sitting in bed in my tiny apartment. It's winter and the wind whines through the windows, the old building creaking. I'm trying to relax and meditate, to quiet the voices in my head telling me I'm a failure. I'm struggling a bit with graduate school; I'm not sure I'm studying the right thing, but the course of study has provided me with a scholarship that's paying for school. I've always been told I need to work hard and be a success, but I'm butting up against this feeling again, the one I've had since I was a little girl, that there must be more to life than just hard work. My siblings don't seem to have this problem and they are both already more successful than me, having advanced in their careers while I was in the Peace Corps and then traveling. I'm feeling like a lost loser and hoping that meditation will give me the answers I can't seem to find.

The angel blobs routinely show up now. I've kept a journal off and on since I was a little girl, so I start making notes of what I'm feeling before and after they appear. I'm not asking questions or interacting with them yet, but as they come closer and become more distinct, the love and light beaming from them gets stronger. Even as I fear being rejected or judged by them, the love I feel is too amazing to deny.

They sometimes merge into one ring of light so that I'm encased in a donut—or, more appropriately for Minnesota, a Bundt cake—of yummy love. Answers to questions start coming into my mind when I'm writing and through my dreams. My practice isn't structured, but it provides comfort. I get used to having the angels around and continue to soak up their love, frequently crying from the pure power of it. I didn't tell anyone, though, for years. I don't want anyone to question it, so it's just between me and them. It feels too good for me to have someone tell me I must be making it up, and why would angels hang out with me?

How does all of this apply to you? Once we go over the ways you might receive guidance, you may realize that you've already been getting it, and we can build upon that. You may also feel like you're not going to get guidance, because why would they bother with you? If that's the case, please just try. You are worthy of all good things coming to you, including love and support. We all are.

You don't have to get specific answers to questions to be bathed in love, either; it just flows from your guides because their role is to help you feel it. And you might find that it's just as good as answers to your questions.

In this chapter, we'll go over the basic steps for setting up a safe space, scripts you can use to start interacting with your guides, and what might come up as we begin. The guides will build upon what's already working, just as they did with me and my journaling. The more you pay attention to ways you may already be receiving guidance, the easier it will be for that to continue and for other avenues of communication to strengthen.

None of this is precise and everything can be adapted to you, what feels good, and what helps you get results with ease and joy.

HOW GUIDANCE SHOWS UP

BREADCRUMBS AND BURIED TREASURE, THAT'S how I think of this. Your guides are always with you, ready to help, so we're just starting the conversation and helping to move it along. The guidance comes as nudges, intuitions, hunches. It can be very subtle—more like hints than hits on the head.

You don't have to be good at visualization or meditation for this to work. How does this inner voice, this guidance, show up for you? For me, it's a very quiet, gentle voice that usually asks a question about doing something differently—or it's a bad feeling in my stomach or my heart that something's wrong and I need to pay attention right now. Our bodies carry a lot of wisdom, so think of how guidance might feel as well as how it might show up in your thoughts.

In Chapter 1, I mentioned some of the ways that guidance comes for me and my students. Here is a more comprehensive list of how you might experience it.

- You get goose bumps when angels or other guides are around. Many people do. It happens to me sometimes when I'm talking to someone, which tells me that a message for them may be coming in.
- You feel pressure in your shoulder blades, where your wings would be if you had them.

- You feel nervous excitement in your stomach.
- You feel a pleasant warmth in your heart (nothing scary or heart palpitations).
- You suddenly feel expansive, positive, or filled with light (this is hard to describe!).
- You wake up with a song going through your head, and the lyrics relate to something you're wondering about (this happens to me a lot).
- Someone important to you, famous or a mentor, comes to you in a dream. You might get a direct message from this person, or their presence might be part of a message.
- You keep seeing the same numbers, 12:12 on a clock, for instance, and find that what you're doing at those moments is important. The appearance of these numbers can also mean that your guides are with you.
- You overhear a conversation—while waiting in line for a coffee or lunch, for example—that answers a specific question you've had.
- Books fall off shelves in front of you, or you remember a book you'd forgotten you have and find it quickly.
- You consistently smell perfume, roses, or some other scent. This can indicate the presence of a specific guide or an ancestor. For a decade or so after the birth of my children, my father showed up from time to time. With him, it was the smell of cigarettes (no one I know smokes, but he did so it was obvious).
- Emails or online notifications come up for something you've really wanted without you having to look for it. I've enrolled in several courses this way or learned about someone with the expertise I'm looking for.

- You notice that people around you are talking about something you've wanted to do but haven't, and they weren't interested in that thing before. This happened for me with painting after my divorce: suddenly, multiple people in my life were interested in learning to paint and just kept talking about it. I'd been feeling the urge to do it myself, but I'd never studied and didn't know how to start. Once I finally got some paints and canvases, none of them ever mentioned painting again. I learned great lessons of surrender in the painting process that helped me work with my guides more deeply.
- You feel a strong resonance in your heart and body when in the presence of what feels like truth. When I read about a course I should take or recognize a dream I should follow, it makes me cry or takes my breath away and I feel an immediate need for it. It's almost like my spine lines up, clicks into place like a row of LEGOs.

Which of these already applies to you? I bet you've experienced more than one. If not, it's probably because the guidance you're receiving is subtle and you're not used to noticing it. How did you find this book? Your guides helped get you here, so look at how that happened.

INNER CRITICS

BEFORE WE GO ANY FURTHER, I need to point out that we all have inner critics—the nagging voices on autopilot that jump in to tell us how much we suck, how we're unworthy of good things happening, how we don't know what we're doing and never will, etc. We *all* have them. It's part of having a brain, apparently. There are many studies on this and books that go into how to deal with them (one of my favorites is *Playing Big* by Tara Mohr).

I've struggled with inner critics my whole life. They come from childhood or the media or wherever. I usually don't try to engage them; I try to shut them up. Sometimes it works to just beam love all over them, sort of like syrup on pancakes, so they are smothered in love and quiet down.

Everything you read in this book originally came from my trying to silence them, so in some ways, I'm grateful for the struggles that started me on this path of working with my guides.

You're not a terrible person because your inner voices tell you that. You can create ways to communicate with your guides to get the comfort and clarity you're looking for, even if your inner critics are intent on judging or shaming you or telling you you're not good enough to get guidance. We'll get there, step by step, in the next few chapters.

THE BASIC STEPS

THE BEST WAY TO START talking to your guides is whatever comes from your heart and feels comfortable to do. Just start the basic conversation with a welcome, how you'd say hi to someone you'd like to be friends with. You're simply setting the intention and saying hi. We'll keep adding details as you read through the book or listen to it, but this starts the process and lets your guides know that you're ready to receive more.

There are four small steps to getting started. If you like to dance, you can think of them as a dance. This sequence will quickly become natural and something you can do in a minute or two. I'll list the steps and then go into the details.

- Take three deep breaths.
- Get grounded.
- Create a safe space.
- Set your intention to get great support.

Is it critical that you do these steps? No. In fact, most people who teach meditation don't go into them. So why do I? Because they help you get ready to sense guidance, focus your attention and energy, and help you trust what you're sensing in only a minute or two if you use the process outlined here. Now I'll go through each step in more detail.

Take three deep breaths.

You won't always need to do this, but it's good to get into the habit as it's the number one thing you can use to quickly calm yourself down and it can be done anywhere. Take a deep breath, one that fills up your belly. Hold it for a count of three or so, let it out slowly (or puff it out loudly if you're tense or upset; the puffing seems to carry negative energy out of your body), rest for a count of three, and then repeat the process two more times. I find that by the end of the third breath, my head feels clearer and my body feels calmer.

This is the breathing process I use, and it works for me, but an early reader pointed me to the book *Breath* by James

Nestor and the breathing exercises noted there. If you already use deep breathing techniques, or if you find a practice such as those shared in *Breath* that brings you clarity and a feeling of calm peace in your body, go ahead and substitute that for what I described. For now, let's assume that you will use this or another approach to gain the calming benefits of a deep breathing practice.

Get grounded.

A lot of us aren't grounded most of the time. What does this mean? In a nutshell, we need to get out of our heads and into our bodies and hearts. How do we do that? There are many ways to try, but here's one that works well for many of my students: Stand up and imagine that you're a tree and roots are coming out of your feet, into the earth, going down at least three feet into the soil. Feel how that both anchors and centers you.

Another way is to imagine there are magnets on the soles of your feet pulling you to the earth (a bit too mechanical for me, but it might work great for you). Playing with modeling clay is grounding, too, or putting your hands into the soil around a house plant. It's all about your connection to the planet, so this is part of the reason putting your bare feet on the ground or on a sandy beach feels so good.

I don't know exactly how to explain what being grounded feels like. For me, it feels more settled, calm, and centered. It's not a strong physical sensation, like a pull, but rather that I don't feel like my energy is shooting off all over the place. My body appreciates this lower level of internal chaos. Play with grounding and see what works for you.

We're on the planet and part of her energy field. It makes sense that we should feel grounded, settled, centered in our bodies, and connected to the planet as part of feeling secure. When I'm feeling grumpy for seemingly no reason and can't figure out why, most of the time, it's related to not being grounded in some way.

Whatever method you use to do this, do it every day, a couple of times a day, until you get used to how it feels when you're grounded. It makes a huge difference in your outlook.

You know those people who are kind of space heads (that's my wording) and like to talk about spiritual things but seem way too floaty about it? They aren't grounded.

The point of being in a human body isn't to keep wishing that you weren't or to float off into the stars and dream. The point is to experience the light and love of your soul and to share your joy, gifts, and love as best you can while in your body.

Gaining spiritual mastery isn't about expanded states of consciousness, it's about expanding your ability to love and use your gifts while in the body. That's why starting off grounded is so important.

Create a safe space.

This means making sure that you're someplace where you feel physically safe and free of distractions while you focus inward or close your eyes. It also means ensuring that you are protected from negative energies and only call in guides of the highest light.

Making sure you're physically safe doesn't need to be a big deal if you're only reaching out to your guides with a quick request, like when you're looking for a parking space. If you're making a longer request or just want to spend time in peaceful energy, then do it in a private place where your physical safety is not a concern.

If you've survived physical trauma or abuse, then take extra time with this. Your mind and body may be on high alert, your adrenals ready for flight, so learning to feel safe will be important so you can relax enough to sense guidance. For most of us, this can be done quickly, but do check and make sure your body isn't holding energy that keeps you tense or part of your system on high alert. Take as long as you need to play with this, but once you have an approach down, this part of the process can be done in a minute or two. You can, of course, ask the guides to help you create a safe space if this is something you struggle with.

Calling upon guides for your highest good might take a bit more practice, but don't worry, there are scripts below for this. You may try several of the approaches shared to find what's best for you. The point of this step is to make sure you are surrounded by high-level energy only, that you only communicate with guides of the highest light and love, and that you receive guidance that's filled with clarity and comfort, and easily perceived and understood.

I'd just started recognizing the presence of angels when I became aware of ghosts or disembodied spirits hanging around, most of them related to my ex-husband's family. Many of these people were holding onto fears or other negative emotions and I didn't necessarily want to hear from them. Just because someone is no longer in their body doesn't mean they are wise or have your highest good in mind. I just decided to leapfrog over that plane of existence and only work with guides of higher light.

I strongly recommend that you include this step as part of the standard way you open communication with guides. If you feel an affinity with disembodied spirits or would like to interact with a specific ancestor, just make sure you're energetically safe when you work with them. The steps below will support that.

Knowing you're safe and trusting your guides helps you surrender to their guidance and release mental constraints that limit your options. The point is to access higher wisdom while you're here, in your body and functioning on the planet, not to use meditation and work with guides to avoid living your life and dealing with your issues.

It's easy to stop interactions with any energies that don't feel right when you first start to reach out for guidance. You clearly state, "I set the intention to be surrounded and supported by only my guides of highest light. I call upon these guides to clear my energetic space of all lower energies now."

We are embodied souls and have the right to feel safe. Using a strong request to your guides that is supported by your intention when establishing a boundary or your safety is part of your free will, and the guides will respect this.

I've included scripts at the end of this chapter to help with this.

Set your intention to receive great guidance.

Set an intention to receive guidance in an easy and recognizable way, and it will happen. You can do this right now, just say the following: "I intend to receive clear guidance that's easy to understand and follow." Does that feel like it's not enough, or like it can't be powerful or important if it's simple? If so, just keep reading or listening—we'll dig into all of this so that it feels more real.

Start with the expectation that learning to sense (hear, feel, or see) your guidance will take a while. You're developing deep friendships that you can count on; these relationships always take time and can also feel joyous right from the start. No one, including me, just starts having great interactions with their guides. Like any deep friendship, it's worth the effort.

ARE YOU OPEN TO BEING GUIDED?

THIS IS A GOOD TIME to check in with yourself: are you open to being guided? Did fears about not being able to do this, not being ready, it being too much work, etc., come jumping in as soon as we got to specifics? That's the case for many of the students I've worked with, and it was something I had to work on when I started. The guides address these concerns in a question-and-answer section in the next chapter, but it's helpful to gut check yourself right now.

Yes, it can be scary to start. Yes, it will take time and commitment, and fears or other limiting beliefs will come up along the way. Dealing with outdated beliefs and fears will be part of the process the whole time you work with guides (and it's part of being human, even without their support; we are always coming up against fears or internal issues). I call this peeling the onion: you make progress on one outdated feeling or belief and another one comes up to be released.

It's all good, it's just helpful to be aware of what's going on inside you so you can face or release it and keep moving forward.

Learning to trust the guidance you're getting is critical. I still don't pay attention at times when my fears want me to hide, or my inner critics convince me my work has no value, or my mind thinks it already knows the best approach. It's normal.

I don't tend to differentiate between my intuition (which to me is guidance from my soul and tends to be felt in my body) and support from my guides (which tends to come in as a quiet voice) because all this guidance is for my well-being. The point is that it's not coming from my brain, it's not saying negative things to me, and it's all too easy to ignore.

The point is to catch yourself and open up so your guides can help. Our subconscious is sneaky and will keep coming up with ways to hold us back, so paying attention to our tension and focusing on our intention to receive the clarity and comfort we're seeking will help us sit in that state of being open to guidance.

There's nothing wrong with some healthy skepticism. If it's helpful, you can adopt a scientific approach to doing this work, treating suggestions as experiments to see what happens. I worked as an environmental scientist for thirty-five years, so I'm used to taking this approach to life. There's no harm in trying things out to see if they make sense for you and revising them as best for you. I'm pragmatically spiritual—I believe in what works—so go ahead and test everything out so you can feel these steps working for you, too.

Let's start with the basic assumption that guidance is available and all around you. You can ask the guides to give you a sign that they are with you and then watch for a few days. Many people start finding feathers on the sidewalk in front of them when their angel guides are around. Others start seeing hearts on everything, including in tree bark, or finding heart-shaped rocks. Ask your guides to help you find a parking space, or to help you find your keys or your phone (sadly, I use that request often). A series of synchronicities can be the guides, trying to get you to notice them—the improbable odds work to get our attention.

Dive in using the notes and scripts at the end of this chapter. Try one script for a few days and note whatever you sense. If it doesn't work, try something else. Taking notes of what you asked and what happened helps you see the results.

I'll tell you, though, it's best at some point to move away from testing them and just get on with assuming they're around, asking for help, and then expressing thanks when it comes. After a while, it becomes second nature to ask for help and then say thank you.

FROM THE GUIDES

Are these steps necessary?

No, but they make the process more efficient and enjoyable and are built upon a framework you can trust. Although we are here to support you, we understand that you may not believe or trust that you're worthy of a bunch of angels giving you hugs and support. We get it, so go ahead and approach this work as feels comfortable for you. Just know we are still all around you and ready to help as much as you'll let us.

Do I need to use the exact words in these scripts?

Not at all. No precise words or actions are needed. These are guidelines only; you can create your own process and choose which words to use. The intention to work with your guides and ask for help is more powerful than any words.

TRY THIS

You can use these simple scripts to get started. Change the wording as feels most comfortable for you and make note of it to use later. We will build upon these initial steps to create a process template for you in Chapter 6. For now, it's more important to just begin.

- Get grounded: Imagine roots growing from your feet into the ground, or magnets on the soles of your feet holding you steady on the planet.
- Create a safe space: Say, "I intend to work only with spirit guides of the highest love, and to always be in a safe space when working with my guides."
- Set your intention: "I intend to reach out to my spirit guides to get answers, and to be open to getting guidance and understanding what's being shared. I know this will be a back-and-forth process that takes time to work out. I intend for this process to feel joyful and supportive."
- Ask something. It can be something specific or general. Here are some examples:
  - "I ask my guides to walk with me through my day and help me feel their presence."

- ◦ "I ask for help dealing with my grumpy coworker today."
- ◦ "I ask for help knowing how best to stay patient with my kids today."
- ◦ "I ask for help dealing with my health concerns."
- ◦ "I ask for answers to how I can find more money to get through each month."

Over the next few days, pay attention to what you notice or feel that's different. If you feel comforted, or get goose bumps, or think some new ideas come from them, for example, say thanks and let them know. It's easier to start the flow of information if they know what catches your attention.

TYPES OF GUIDES

EVERY CLIENT AND STUDENT I'VE worked with has more than one type of guide, but most of us begin with an affinity for or interest in a particular figure. This primary relationship may be the only one you are interested in, with other guides remaining in the background until some future time (or never).

Back at the beginning of my journey, I spent a lot of time trying to quiet my inner critics (and get help to do this). I found a book on Kuan Yin, the Buddhist goddess, or bodhisattva, of compassion, and felt a strong connection to her, having traveled through Nepal and Thailand on my way home from the Peace Corps. I prayed to her for guidance and felt great comfort and acceptance from her presence after some time. In everything I read, she always seemed so peaceful and loving, so accepting of whatever flaws anyone had. This was the first guide I actively reached out to; I struggled for years to feel comfortable with the presence of the angels, as I couldn't accept that they wanted to help me. This probably came from my Lutheran upbringing; God didn't seem very forgiving or supportive, at least not the God I heard about in sermons, and the emphasis was on asking for forgiveness of our sins. I was always afraid the angels would see the truth about me and judge me. Who wants that from Archangel Michael? Better to keep a bit of distance.

Since we all have a bunch of guides who can provide support in multiple ways, it's helpful to have an idea of who you might call upon for assistance or who you feel may already be with you. Let's start with a quick introduction to the types of spirit guides you might be working with. We're wading into the pool, not high diving here.

Working with your guides should feel normal and comforting, not make you nervous. The amount of time needed to sense them varies. Sometimes it can happen as soon as you reach out to them. Or you may never sense them, but instead get external indications they are around and then you can start to assume they're with you.

It's not necessary to know the names of your guides to start working with them. This is something I struggled with when I began; since I'd never heard much about angels, I figured spirit guides were just people who'd died and wanted to help. I thought I had to know their names and be able to imagine what they looked like before I could work with them. That isn't true. Worrying about their names or what they look like is just another way for our minds to tell us we're doing something wrong. It's our intention, not what we call them, that's important.

Some of my students experience contact with their guides the first time we do a practice, and others work with these steps for a while, sometimes weeks, before they begin to sense presences or inputs. There's no right or wrong; use whatever process works for you and your guides. There's no point in having a first experience so intense that you stop doing it. If you're not sensing anything, look for signs in the external world, like feathers and heart shapes or messages on license plates, online ads, or buses.

You might perceive figures while working with your guides, or they might manifest as geometric shapes or without form at all. You may not want to perceive any type of shape, and if that's the case, you can just let them know. Especially at the beginning, it might be too much of a shock to have one of your guides pop up in front of your face when you're just looking for help finding a parking space.

QUICK CHECK-IN

LET'S STOP FOR A SECOND before we move on because you're about to be exposed to a broader range of guides than you may have considered before. This could bring up thoughts about not being worthy of guidance. Or you may think that you won't have these kinds of guides, or more than one guide, and so this can't apply to you. That's normal: we judge ourselves and think the guides will do the same (at least, that's what I've thought many times, and what students and clients have told me).

For the record, I am 100 percent certain that you have not only a guardian angel, but many angels and many other guides working with you. In fact, I keep being shown pictures of them looking over the shoulders of the people reading this book, wanting to help. Cuddling up with you while you listen in bed.

Look at all the chaos going on around us, both locally and on a global scale. This is a powerful time to be a human. Our guides are with us to help us be the best humans we can be so we can make an impact on other people's lives and support the planet, even in small ways. How many times has a smile or a greeting from someone you don't know helped you get through a tough day? We can make major impacts in tiny ways when we strive to be the best we can be.

So it's important to stop the critical inner voices that are starting to shame or judge you. I understand that they will crawl out of the mud and start slinging it at you; it happens to all of us. This work won't change the fact that those voices come back, but you will have support at your back and tools at hand to silence them, and move on when you tap into the guides already sending you love and support. We'll go over ways to silence your inner critics in Chapter 7. For now, let's get back to exploring the different types of guides you might work with.

YOUR GUIDES

IF YOU ALREADY HAVE GUIDES that you call upon and/or include in your prayers or meditations, such as saints, deities, loved ones who have passed, or spiritual teachers, keep working with them. This work will simply augment and support those relationships and practices, not take anything away from them.

If you're looking to connect with your intuition, your own soul's guidance, and don't have much interest in other kinds of guides, everything else in this book still applies.

If you're unsure about the guidance you might get or whether this is real or not and struggle with trust, you can think of all the different types of guides below as archetypes that support the human experience and run with that.

All of this is meant to be helpful in whatever ways work for your heart and mind.

The following list comes from the types of guides I've interacted with over the past thirty-five years personally and with my clients and students. None of them are specific to me or certain groups or types of people—we all get to benefit from them if we want to.

The general types of guides you might work with could include:

- Angels
- Goddesses, gods, saints, or deities
- Spiritual teachers
- Ascended masters or enlightened beings
- Star beings (you might think of these as aliens)
- Ancestor spirits
- Family members who've passed
- Nature spirits
- Your higher self (your soul)

You might find that you also have types of guides that aren't listed above; there are many beings of love and light here now to help us. If a certain kind of guide isn't listed, that doesn't mean it's not a valid kind of guide, just that I haven't worked with them. I'll never claim to have worked with every kind of guide, but the range of guides I work with keeps expanding, which could happen to you as well.

Here are some thoughts on the types of guides I've worked with from the list I shared.

Angels. The angels provide comfort, protection, and a clear sense that you're interacting with the Divine. There are many types of angels and hierarchies you can call upon. People most frequently work with their guardian angel, healing angels, and archangels. This is a broad category of beings who provide healing, protection, and feelings of grace, joy and ease.

Goddesses, gods, saints, or deities. These guides come forward with a particular focus on helping you access their energies, skills, and powers to complete part of your work on the physical plane. As we move away from the old patriarchal energies of punitive power and into a more equitable age, I anticipate that more of these entities will come forward to support us. Many of them were suppressed as part of limitations imposed on our abilities to access our true worth and power, or turned into mythological figures known only through stories.

Star beings (you might think of these as aliens). You may feel you're from another place in the cosmos or are looking for innovative ways to solve problems in society. The star beings bring new energy technologies and wisdom teachings from planetary cultures much older than Earth. We all have these connections, and you can go down a rabbit hole trying to figure them out. It can be easiest to start by asking for help finding innovative solutions to your concerns, as they are great at this. You can also ask for assistance in line with your soul lineage. Some star beings you may have heard of are the Andromedans, Arcturians, and Sirians. My work, especially the work I do to anchor light on the planet, increasingly involves partnering with star beings.

Ascended masters. The ascended masters have significant teachings to share on energy technologies, healing modalities, spiritual growth, embodying your soul essence, and increasing your resonance in support of your divine mission. If the word "masters" is offensive, they can be referred to as enlightened beings, ones who achieved spiritual expertise that they now share with us. Many people will partner with a specific enlightened being for much of their spiritual work, and there are many online resources that provide additional details about these guides. I generally work with them on specific concerns for shorter periods of time.

Ancestors. In many cases, ancestor spirits are not linked to your birth family. They come forward from past lives on this planet and others and can have links to current cultures or global issues. For instance, many people involved in work to support the Earth may have Indigenous elders or shamans as guides who can share their wisdom about living in harmony with the planet. Although I don't have shamanic training in this life, I have shamanic ancestors, both male and female, who work with me. It's important to maintain spiritual integrity around this and not claim expertise—such as calling yourself a shaman—if you haven't trained with traditional shamanic practitioners. As you develop your spiritual practice, you'll notice that people sometimes claim this kind of knowledge or share their ideas of wisdom teachings from ancestors without true experience. Discernment is part of your spiritual path.

Nature spirits. Nature spirits can be particularly helpful if you want a stronger connection to the planet and/or are interested in supporting environmental healing. A key aspect of my energy work is forging new relationships with nature spirits and the elemental kingdom. These guides will be increasingly critical to figuring out how to live more sustainably on the planet, and part of our role as spiritually oriented humans can be to work with these beings to preserve the planet.

Higher self. Your higher self is the part of you that isn't confined to this 3D reality, it is the expanded, wiser, higher-dimensional aspects of your soul. A huge part of our mission in this life involves accessing and embodying more aspects of our higher self, which exists in an expanded state unconstrained by the human body. As we work with our guides, our ability to access our higher self through our intuition and dreams increases. In fact, many people who begin working with a spiritual guide come to realize that it is, in fact, their higher self. All the practices in this book can be used to increase your intuition and your connection to your higher self.

HOW I GET MESSAGES FROM MY GUIDES

I SHARE NOTES FROM MY guides throughout this book, and I want to provide some details on how I receive these messages as I'm always asked about it. Here are the various ways it works for me.

When I'm talking to someone, I will sometimes see an image of something they could do or that I see coming their way.

I'm very visual. When I meditate, I go to my temple of light, my inner sanctuary, and see my guides. It's like I'm in a movie: I meet them, talk with them, walk around with them, and even go on journeys with them sometimes. I also hear what they say and write it down.

I have a Creativity Council I call together to help me write. When I am writing, I see myself in a safari tent in my inner sanctuary. Sometimes I get messages there, and sometimes my guides are just present while I write. I do hear them talking to me when I'm just going through my day sometimes, too, and they are always around (when I can't find my keys, for instance). I just ask for help, and they always bring me what I need.

I'm also a conscious channel for some of my guides. This means that I let them speak through me when I'm giving someone a healing session or a reading. It isn't so much a handing over of my body, or that I'm not present, it's more like when you go someplace with a friend and something happens that makes for a great story, but they are better at telling it, so you let them even though you can jump in and add your bits. It's an extension of the partnership I have with my guides and another way I interact with them as my Family of Light.

I believe in God, Source, Divine Oneness—however we describe it. For me, the guides are aspects of that energy, as we all are. We are all divine at heart, we've just forgotten it as part of our human experience. Each guide conveys an aspect or aspects of Source, and I think their purpose in our lives comes down to helping us remember these divine aspects we carry inside of us as well. We are infinite, powerful beings of love having a brief human experience and then returning to oneness and wholeness.

GOOD SPIRITUAL MANNERS

THERE ARE SEVERAL THINGS TO understand about working with your guides that aren't requirements but will create a solid framework for your communications.

- Treat your guides with respect, as you would any close friends. If you ask them for help, try to sense their guidance. If you don't sense anything, ask them to help you perceive them and for their guidance to be easy to understand. If you do sense something, let them know so they can build upon what's working.
- If you set up a standing time when you will be asking for guidance, say before bed, show up. If you're not sure you can stay with a set time, don't set up that expectation for you or for them. (I'm not good at sticking to a specific time, so I don't set things up that way.) You can always change or revise the expectation but do try to honor your intention.

- Don't ask the guides to do things for or to other people—this work is only for you. In Chapter 8, I will share guidance on how to ask for support for someone in a way that doesn't violate their free will and is for the highest good of all.
- Guidance will never be angry or negative. Ever. In fact, that's one of the best ways to check whether you're making something up: if a message is judgmental, peevish, irritated, or angry, it's not coming from the guides. Please bring a similarly positive energy to them. If you're going through a crisis, it's okay to be agitated and even angry—I've been that way too—but try and dial it back as much as possible. They are always here to help.
- Be grateful for their presence and support, even as you're learning to perceive and understand it.

GRATITUDE

CREATING A SIMPLE GRATITUDE PRACTICE is also a great way to start receiving guidance, since your higher self and guides can come closer to you when your heart is open. Expressing your gratitude is the easiest way to receive regular guidance. Why do I say this? Expressing gratitude for all the gifts in your life puts you in a frame of mind to clearly see your life and those gifts. A gratitude practice changes the way you see the world, and over time you notice more and more to be grateful for.

I sometimes turn this into a game when I'm driving, since I get so grumpy with other drivers: I start saying all the things I'm grateful for and see if I can keep it up nonstop until I reach my destination. I've lived in places where clean air and water aren't a given, so I always start with those, and then give thanks for my kids and my home and all the beauty in my life. Try this. You'll be amazed by how much you have to be grateful for.

Noting what I'm grateful for, especially all the beauty around us and the blessings I get from nature, is a huge part of my spiritual practice. I do this before I go to sleep at night and during the day whenever I notice things. This planet is astoundingly beautiful!

I frequently feel joyful, and I give thanks for this, too. Joy is what I feel the most anymore, a feeling that has developed over the years of hanging out with my guides.

If your inner critic is now jumping all over you about how you don't do this and you're a loser and going to fail: I don't do it every day, and I'm not walking through life singing songs of joy like a cartoon princess. In fact, if I'm ever able to drive my car for ten minutes without thinking that other drivers are jerks (and usually saying so, accompanied by hand signals), I'll probably spontaneously combust. I'm frequently grumpy and ignore my guides, but I've noticed that being grateful brings in more of what I've grateful for, so it's an effective practice that I enjoy.

TRY THIS

Are you drawn to a particular type of guide? Do you already have a prayer practice that includes one or more of the guides I listed? Is there a kind of guide you've always wanted to work with, like an angel or goddess? Ask for their input directly or ask about an issue related to the kind of help they provide.

Have you sensed the presence of any of these guides before, or wondered about specific guides based on things you've read or seen in movies or online? If so, welcome their input on how you can work with them.

Here are some sample questions to use to start the conversation.

- Why am I drawn to this book and working with you now?
- I've always wanted to feel the presence of angels (or substitute from the list)—why is that?
- Can you show me a sign that you are with me?
- How would you like to work with me?
- Is there a best way to start feeling your comfort and guidance?

I think these questions are perfect for walking meditations, especially in a beautiful park or other setting where there's a bit of wild nature to get your thoughts and feelings flowing.

You can also just say, "I want more guidance; I'm open to getting more guidance." You can even say that you're ready for your guides to appear, but you want it to be subtle and gentle (no blazing chariots of light landing in the front yard).

Ask for help. This is a huge deal—just ask. Talk to them; they hear you. Just notice things and then ask for help figuring out what they mean. Ask for help a lot. Be grateful and ask for help! That pretty much takes care of all of it. Now you know how to start having a solid relationship with your guides.

After you've opened the conversation with your question or questions, pay close attention to your thoughts and what appears in front of you over the next few days. Remember, guidance can show up in many ways.

I don't usually sense my guides around me, to be honest. I just know they're there, so I talk to them and ask for help knowing it will come—this takes practice! Keep asking questions or just sharing how you're feeling as you go through your day.

This was a big chapter. We went over a lot of things that might be very new to you. This prep work is critical; you're starting to work with your tools and assembling the pieces of the practice you'll create in the coming chapters. If you're having trouble getting your inner dialogue (or diatribes) to quiet down so you can sense guidance and your intuition, don't worry—we'll cover that in Chapter 6. For now, let's explore some of the ways your guides can help make your dreams come true, some of the best ways of working with them.

CHAPTER 4
DREAMS AND INSPIRATION

I GREW UP IN A town in Iowa of less than a thousand people, where the library was about the size of my living room. Even so, my favorite thing was to walk the three blocks to Main Street, then to the end of the two-blocks-long downtown to find a book, even one I'd read before. I thought writers were real-life wizards, and that I too would write magical stories.

Fast forward a few decades to 2010. We've been in Louisiana for a few years, having moved from the Chicago area the year after Hurricane Katrina so I could do recovery work. The boys are now teenagers and don't need as much of my time. My work with my guides is increasingly powerful, and I work with a range of them beyond just the angelic realm. My inner sanctuary has expanded to include gardens and other buildings, and my experiences there with my guides form the framework of my spiritual life. My journeys there are vivid, and the energies I share with my guides help me feel more confident and resilient in the outer world.

My inner life is exciting and loads of fun, even when I'm releasing old patterns. As a little girl, I dreamed of a life of international adventures. Now my journeys are interstellar, though they happen on the inside.

My work with my guides fills me up, carries me, and sustains me. Apart from releasing old patterns and dealing with limitations, the main aspect of my ongoing spiritual work is the joy I increasingly feel—the bliss that's started to seep from my meditations into my everyday life. The guides nudge me to share my work with others.

I take notes during my meditations and start blogging details of my spiritual adventures in 2011. Many people comment on how the details of my meditations seem like movies to them and have a dreamlike quality. This is deeply affirming: Dreaming with my guides, entering a safe space, and allowing my heart and mind to ramble freely while we work together to make my dreams come true is what I love to do most. The work is juicy, delicious, inspiring, and relaxing at the same time. It pulls me into deeper and deeper partnership with my guides. This is when I start referring to them as my "Family of Light," since they truly do feel like family.

Our guides excel at bringing us inspiration and increasing our creativity since they see our potential and our path from a higher perspective and are here to help us make our dreams come true. In this chapter, we'll go over ways to access that support.

THE GUIDES SEE YOU AND YOUR PATH CLEARLY

OUR GUIDES CAN SEE OUR potential and want to help us bring that potential into our lives. Many times, our biggest dreams were buried when we were told as children to stop believing in things that wouldn't happen. I've found that remnants of buried dreams nudge their way back into our consciousness when it's time for them to come forward. We might see examples of others living that dream or get messages in our nighttime dreams as reminders.

Over the past few decades, it took the help of all the guides I could call in to get me past my fears and limitations so I could become an author, my oldest dream. Guides helped me find writing courses and the money for them, the energy to write when the kids were small, and the software and training to create websites, blogs, courses, and podcasts. I called in goddess guides for creative inspiration, and healing support from angels and star beings when I despaired of ever feeling ready to share my work or make my little girl dreams come true.

There are multiple ways to go about fulfilling your dreams with the help of your guides. One is to get help pursuing a dream you already have. Another is to spend quiet time with your imagination and see what comes up as inspiration for new dreams. Big dreams, little ones, business-related dreams, even finding the perfect recipe to help create a family holiday tradition—it doesn't matter. You can call in guides to help with the specifics without knowing their names or what kinds of guides they are; you just ask for the help you need and make sure to ask that it be easy and joyful at the same time. Getting help to dream big should be fun and freeing.

The dream state is a frame of mind and heart where all possibilities are available and perceived limitations can be released. Using the idea of dreaming moves the mind out of constraint and limitation and into the energy field of potential.

What if you're not sure what your dreams are? You can ask for help remembering dreams you buried, or expanding on what you think might be possible. Movies or books might be good inspirations in this instance: is there a theme among the stories you love? Look for the hints in your life.

Walking meditation is great for entering a dream state that moves past mental ideas of what's possible, as is journaling. Using visuals from magazines or social media feeds can inspire new visions of what you'd love to create or experience. There are some great books on using your imagination and staying playful included in the recommended resources on my website at Julesapollo.com/extras. The point of working with the guides is to move beyond what you think and into the power of bigger possibilities that come through your heart and connection to your guides and your expanded self.

USING YOUR GUIDES' ENERGY TO FUEL YOUR DREAMS

DREAMING IS WHERE YOU REALLY begin to experience the power of working with your guides, and it's all based on being in harmony, or resonance, with them. What does that mean? Basically, when your energy—the frequency of your being—lines up with theirs, you're in harmony. Our guides have frequencies too. I love to go into old cathedrals when they're empty, sit in silence, and absorb the calm and higher frequencies anchored in the air and stones from centuries of voices raised in praise. If you get goose bumps when your guides are around, it's a sign that you're perceiving higher frequencies.

We've all walked into rooms where the vibe feels good and we're instantly comfortable. I seem to always feel this in older bookstores with lots of comfy seats to sink into. You might have felt this around the fireplace in the living room of a friend's home or in a kitchen filled with laughter and people you love.

We all emit frequencies of light as part of the electromagnetic system in our bodies. When you spend time with your guides (whether you're consciously aware of their presence or not), you're in the presence of higher frequencies. Over time, you entrain to those frequencies; in essence, your vibration rises to resemble that of your guides more closely. I'm not making this up—the idea of frequency entrainment is used in physics. The archangels' vibration is higher than ours. The frequency of a goddess is different from that of an archangel, but still higher than ours. The energies of different guides may feel a bit different, but they are all higher frequencies than we usually encounter when we're interacting with other humans.

I mention this because after working with your guides for a while, you'll notice that it's easier for you to sense their presence, that you get answers and results more quickly, and that you feel generally happier and calmer. This is because your frequency—the vibration of light you emit and share with the world—is higher, filling you with more love, compassion, and joy. I know this to be true because it's been part of my life for several decades, and I've seen it in every single person I've helped to work with their guides.

A higher frequency is not something to strive for. It develops as you release old patterns and expand your heart and mind to feel more joy. A big part of being in harmony with your guides is feeling more joy, as it's such a high frequency. Here's a note from them about joy:

Never doubt the clarion call of your joy—follow it in each moment, whether for comfort, adventure, learning, or laughter, and you will be effortlessly brought to all that you need and desire.

WHAT IF YOU CAN'T IMAGINE ANY DREAMS?

IF YOU'RE IN A TRAUMATIC time or struggling to get by, you may not be able to articulate exactly what you'd like to be different or how things would be if they were ideal. Maybe you struggle to imagine how you'd feel if things were better. The guides can help with this, as well as give you glimpses of your greater potential and possibilities. Here's a script to start with.

"I call upon all my guides of highest light and love and my higher self. I'm having trouble imagining what my dreams are, how things could get better, and how I might feel once they are. Please help me sense what's possible for me that I can't see now. Please bring me images and inspiration for better times, ways I can be more at ease, and ways I can see and experience more of my potential. Please bring all of this with ease, grace, flow, and joy. Hold me in your light and love and help me release anything that holds me back from imagining and realizing my dreams and my full potential. I am so grateful for your help. Thank you."

ASKING FOR HELP

LIKE ANYTHING ELSE YOU'RE WORKING on or want support for, going after your dreams is something you can do with the help of your guides. Here's a simple script to use:

"I call upon all my guides of highest light and my creative muses. Please support me in making my dream come true by sharing inspiration regarding details of this dream, actions to take in support of the dream, and the energy and commitment to follow through on making this dream come true. I am open to receiving guidance on how to make this dream even better than I've imagined. I ask to be filled to the brim with inspiration and held in love while I'm dreaming. I'm grateful for the support."

Details on ways to explore more support are included in the "Try This" section at the end of the chapter.

"WHAT IF?" AND "HOW GOOD CAN I LET IT BE?"

SOMETIMES MY DREAMS ARE CONSTRICTED by what I think is possible, what I've been told I could have, or what's happened before. This constraint is unnecessary and something the guides can help you blow past. One way to deal with it is to ask the questions "What if?" and "How good can I let it be?" I find that the answers I get to these questions are especially expansive if I ask them while doing something relaxing, like sitting in a warm bath or a beautiful garden.

Here's an example. Let's say you're looking for a new job. You could think about the kind of job you want and the place you'd like to work, then ask questions that help create what you want but also expand your ideas of what is possible.

"What if I liked my coworkers? What if I got a great raise? What if I got to use all my skills? What if my boss and the teams I worked with recognized and respected my skills and experience? What if I had flexible hours or could work at home? What if I worked someplace where I could take a walk in a park at lunch? What if there were great opportunities for me to advance in the company?"

You can do this with anything you dream about: having more money to pay bills, resolving your health issues, finding the perfect partner, living in a great place, etc.

The same goes for "How good can I let it be?" Let's say you have dreams of starting a business so you don't need to work for anyone else, and you're thinking about what that could be. You consider the skills you have and what you could offer that people might want—but do you think of what would bring you the greatest joy? What could you create that would bring you not only financial freedom but also the kind of wealth that gives you sovereignty in life and complete freedom in *all* your decisions?

Don't stop reading now just because you think that will never be possible. Imagine—that's all we're doing here. What if you could be sovereign in your life, making decisions with a focus on joy and freedom? What would that feel like? Again, just dream and expand what you imagine might be possible. Try on what that would feel like and how you'd move through your day if it was your reality, and then make it even better. How yummy can you let it feel when your dreams come true? Of course, ask your guides to help you with this; that's the whole point of this chapter. See the "Try This" section for scripts.

Play with these questions and approaches to see if what you're imagining can get even better. Your soul might want things that your mind never thought you could obtain.

FROM THE GUIDES

The following guidance uses beauty and peace to amplify your dreams. It mentions joy, too. Joy is a high-frequency emotion, so combining it with your intention to create plus the power of dreaming in collaboration with your guides makes rocket fuel, here's a message from them.

Imagine yourself in a place of natural beauty. You might be sitting on a sandy beach, in a tent or a cabin in the woods, or under a waterfall. You might be floating around a beautiful lake. You can imagine whatever you want.

Set the intention that you are grounded, connected to the planet. Your connection to nature in this beautiful, peaceful place, combined with light from your soul and your guides, anchors you to the Earth and makes all your dreams manifest much more quickly, easily, and substantially.

We would like you to play with this kind of visualization. It's a way to fill your energy work with light and joy. In contrast with the heavy energies of stress, worry, and tension in your life, using your imagination to create joyfully is the most powerful choice you can make right now.

I get grounded and connect with nature in my garden a lot. I love being around the trees, and I'm able to access my soul and guides' energy more easily when I'm sitting in my backyard sanctuary, feeling vast expansions of possibility dancing in my brain and my heart.

Making sure I'm not limiting how much joy I feel is a big part of dreaming. Feeling bliss is part of the way I feel free. Bliss to me is a subversive emotion, a stealthy way of breaking the paradigm of economic suppression and burden that so many people feel on this planet. Thinking of myself as a spiritual rebel, busting the dominant, suppressive paradigm with my dreaming, makes it even more fun for me.

I've lived and worked in places where life is difficult for many, and I consider it part of my duty as embodied light (that's how I see us all—embodied light) to anchor joy and bliss, and to experience the feeling of freedom in my life, so those states of being contribute to the energy stream of humanity. I believe that each time we feel higher emotions such as love, bliss, joy, and creative freedom, it adds to the wealth of those emotions on the planet. Drops in the bucket, yes, but to me it feels important and increasingly so in these chaotic times.

When I was a little girl, I was a ball of giggly joy even though things were sometimes rough at home—a bit too joyful for some, maybe: I won the fourth grade giggle contest (held because our teacher couldn't get us to shut up). I was also voted as having the "best sense of humor" in my senior class (I tied with a boy whose name I've now forgotten). My sense of humor is a cornerstone of my personality, so when I can't find the humor in a situation, I'm likely to call in extra help from the guides to get back to that.

As we become more heart-centered, we become better able to envision, create, and empower our lives. We can call in our power and create the world of our dreams. We are experts at this; we create our reality and the world we live in through our thoughts and actions every day. We're just not used to thinking of it that way.

HOW I DREAM WITH MY GUIDES

DREAMING AND PLAYING WITH POSSIBILITIES is probably the most fun I have with my guides. Our imaginations are made for this. Here are some of the ways I do it.

Asking "What if?"

This is one of my favorite ways to expand the possibilities I'm thinking about. You can ask the guides to help you see beyond what you think could happen and the ways you limit the dream. For example, I use "what if" when I dream of writing a book. What if the book is easy to write? What if I enjoy marketing it? What if the book is magnetic to its perfect readers? What if it changes people's lives? What if I enjoy both the writing and the editing? What if the process of writing brings wonderful people into my life to help me with all the things I don't know how to do? Anywhere I feel myself getting stuck, I use "what if" to lay out the energy of no longer being stuck and I ask the guides to help make it happen.

Trying it on.

This is similar to the "what if" work but takes it a step further: I'm trying on the identity of the person I want to become. For example, if I'm trying to feel more confident, I think about someone who is confident and how they move through their day. How would I think about my website, my writing, my body, the use of my time, etc., if I was confident in my skills and how to best share them with the world? What can I learn from studying confident artists I admire, like Georgia O'Keeffe, Beryl Markham, Agatha Christie, and Rihanna? How would they go after their dreams? How would they drink their coffee and plan out their day? How would they make time for creativity and prioritize their dreams? Little choices and changes we make when we return to these questions routinely can expand our lives in big ways.

When I write, and while I'm trying on these energies, I call in my Creativity Council and get their help with old limiting patterns that pop up ("Who do you think you are? Someone like you can't write a book anyone wants to read. You have nothing to share that's worth reading…"). I jump on them with the guides right away and keep doing the imagining. I check in throughout the day: What does my successful author self have for dinner? How does she structure her day? When does she take breaks, pay bills, and do laundry? This works for losing weight, managing money, running a business—everything, really.

What I love about this approach is that it brings in my body's wisdom (which is easy for us to ignore). I can feel the reaction in my body when I see myself as a beloved author, talking to a group. How does my body feel when I think about it? Do my shoulders scrunch up, for instance? If so, I work on whatever energy is driving me to shrink. Then I can return to dreaming.

Tent work.

Most of my dreams relate to exploring and sharing my creativity. I have a big tent in my inner sanctuary where I go to write that looks out over a savannah. There's nothing much in the tent except a writing desk, a chair, and some benches and pillows around the perimeter. I call forth my Creativity Council when I'm working on a project, guides who can help me with my writing from beginning concepts through setting up a successful book launch.

You don't have to see your guides or know their names to do something similar; just make sure you call in the guides who will be most helpful. Yes, this is all imagined, but to me, that doesn't matter. I believe in what works for me, and this does.

Road trip with the guides.

I find that some of my best ideas come when I'm on a road trip, or even on short drives while I'm running errands. Any kind of travel works (calling it a road trip makes my inner adventurer smile). And walking the dog, especially when I'm out in a park, works the same way. It's great for getting details on the next steps to take with creative projects. I even tell my guides to ride with me for long trips. I often imagine Archangel Michael in the seat next to me and other guides filling the backseat.

On these trips, I call in my guides, think about something I'm working on or stuck on, and have a back-and-forth conversation: I tend to ask questions out loud as it feels more like a conversation, and I will say out loud what I'm sensing from them to help me mull it over. (You don't need to do this, it's just the way that's most fun for me.) For some reason, it's easier for me to sense an answer and hear the quiet voice of inspiration or intuition when some type of movement is happening.

I'm relaxed in both the asking and the expectation of an answer, knowing that help will come and that it doesn't need to be right then. I don't go after my dreams in isolation, or through talking with my guides one time and then tackling the rest of the work without input. I'm lazy and don't like to waste my time or energy, so I call in all my guides, check in with them, take action that feels good, let go of anything limiting me, and repeat it all.

TRY THIS

Here's an easy script to use to ask your guides for inspiration and to help you make your dreams come true. You can start with a specific dream, like a vacation, or a broader dream like starting your own business while you're still figuring out exact details to focus on.

"I am dreaming of (whatever), and I ask my guides to help me make it real. I ask for guidance related to specific steps, and for help in imagining what might be even better than I've thought possible. If this dream is not for my highest good, please give me gentle nudges toward what is better. I ask to be cocooned in a dreaming state in the comfort of your presence. Thank you."

Here are some ideas for jump-starting your imagination and dreaming.

- Take a vision vacation in a peaceful place (imagined or real), adding in as many details of the completed dream or vision as possible. Use your senses to fill in details to help it feel complete: what are you smelling, seeing, tasting, feeling when your dream's real?
- Do the "What if?" and "How good can I let it be?" exercises for expansive possibilities.

- Fill your creative well with art, music, or movies. Bring your guides along. This concept of an "Artist Date" comes from Julia Cameron's book *The Artist's Way*. I try to do this once a week, even if it's just spending time looking at images or videos. To me, that's a beauty break and it helps replenish me.
- Keep a journal by your bed and track your dreams. Write down a question or something you'd like guidance on before you go to sleep and any dreams you remember when you wake up.

Can you see how the tools we've gone over so far will support you in trusting the guidance you receive and getting help with your dreams? Once you move past the initial dreaming stage and start taking action inspired by your dreams, you're ready to work with your guides to accomplish your goals. That's what we'll cover in the next chapter.

CHAPTER 5
GUIDES AND GOALS

AUGUST 2008. WE'VE BEEN IN Louisiana for two years, and the engineering company I'm working for has reorganized three times in the eighteen months I've worked there. The company isn't doing well, and the office feels increasingly tense.

Then the four of us who make up the environmental department are all laid off in one day. The company has reorganized again and plans to outsource all its environmental work.

I'm not from Louisiana, I don't have a lot of contacts here, and Baton Rouge doesn't have many options for environmental work. I have a big mortgage and three tall sons who need a lot of food every day.

I don't even tell the kids what's happened. I go home, fix supper, and then retreat to my bedroom for an intensive meditation with all my guides. I set up the energy and support to find a job within the next two weeks. I get that in motion first and then start looking at ads and reaching out to contacts. I don't entertain worries or fears; there's no time for that. Every time I start to worry, I call in the guides, set the intention to find a new job, and then keep looking, taking whatever actions feel right. I have two interviews by the end of the first week, and a verbal offer the next. I start working again before my three weeks' worth of severance pay is gone.

I was a project manager for many years, and I tend to approach my own goals in the same way: giving assignments, setting deadlines, and expecting results. I do this for easy things, like finding the right repair company when I need it, and for tougher problems, like dealing with family issues that need immediate results. I've used the same method to find a new house several times. I set the intention to find a home that fits us as a family, is within my budget, keeps us safe, provides easy access to the places we go to most often, and is available when we need it. I tell the guides that I need them to help me find this house quickly, easily, and without stress.

When we moved to Louisiana for my work related to Hurricane Katrina recovery, the housing market was insanely hot. Many people were moving north from New Orleans, and new houses were being purchased above the asking price before they were built. I flew down to Baton Rouge to look for a house with only two days to find one. My company had set me up with a local real estate agent and I'd let her know what I was looking for, but she was clear that it would be tough to find a place and we'd need to act quickly. We looked at two houses in a small town in between Baton Rouge and New Orleans, took a lunch break, and looked at another one under construction. By the end of that day, I'd talked to a loan officer, put in an offer, and had my offer accepted. The kids enjoyed the house-hunting day, capped off with burgers and a swim in the hotel pool, and the agent was astounded by how easy it had been.

I've repeated this process two more times, each time finding what I wanted in a way that felt joyful. The last time was in another hot market, and I was on a tight timeline to find a place that fit our move-out deadline. I didn't tell the guides specifics about neighborhoods or what the house needed to look like, I just gave them details on how we live as a family and how I wanted the home to feel. The how, where, and what I left up to them; my part was to hold the energy of success, stay open to viewing places I might not normally have considered, and act decisively when I found something that fit. It's this kind of partnering that makes life feel magical. My guides and I go after my goals together, as a team.

The great thing about this approach is that you don't have to know how things will get done—you give the guides an assignment and let them figure out how to do it. You remain focused on what you want to get done. The "what" is your part, and the "how" is theirs.

Once you have a working process for communicating with your guides, you can use their help to reach your goals in both general and specific ways, even if you don't have a strong sense of their presence. Think of them as a support system that gives you both a framework for decision-making and details on how to complete individual tasks that will help you realize your vision.

Your guides can support and amplify your efforts and help you decide on the next steps or best choices, but the decision to do something, and the actions required to move forward with what you want, come from you. Your guides help sustain the effort and bolster your confidence in your ability to complete it. That is where your partnership really kicks in.

There are a lot of similarities between how you go about this and how you get general support for your dreams, but the difference here is setting an intention and carrying out the actions. All the tools discussed earlier—intention, imagination, and energy—apply here with additional focused energy because you have a targeted intention. This is where you can best apply the whole toolkit I'm sharing this in this book to identify what you need, to ask for what you specifically need help with, and to let the guides figure out how to get it done.

You can ask the guides to help you be efficient with your time and how you approach defining the goal: breaking it down into steps, revising as you go along, and prioritizing the work. You can also ask specifically for guides of efficiency and those with the energy to jump in and help; you don't need to know their specific names or types.

You're doing the work you'd usually do to accomplish something but asking for support and inspiration along the way, so you get into a flow of ideas and action more easily and are energetically supported by the guides as you're doing it.

You can apply the same approach to big goals related to health, wealth, or love, and to targeted goals such as updating a page on your website or designing and planting a peaceful garden—even tiny things like quickly getting in and out of the DMV when you renew your driver's license. In fact, turning something that's usually painful (like renewing a driver's license) into an easy—dare I say fun—exercise brings me great joy. I feel triumphant when these little victories happen, and ready to look for more ways to make situations easier.

One of the miracles of this work is that it provides you with so much more time to pursue your goals. You might set an intention to prepare for efficient interactions with agencies or banks, for instance, to remove the stress and time usually needed for mundane activities. This can feel so magical and playful that it makes me laugh, and it's another way I know my guides are around, even when I don't sense them.

Here are some examples of things the guides can help bring to you:

- Mentors
- Programs or new teachings so you can gain necessary skills
- Innovative ideas
- New collaborative partners
- Money or time to pursue your goals
- Access to specialists and experts
- Revelations of limiting beliefs that are blocking your success
- Visions of how to complete your goals
- Synchronicities of all kinds, like meeting people or hearing about opportunities.

When I teach a class or work with clients one-on-one, their experiences convince them that working with their guides to reach their goals is bringing them concrete results. Examples they have shared with me include:

- Finding not only mentorship programs, but also paid mentorships offered by the exact program they wanted but didn't think they could get into
- New approaches and experts coming to help with a family member's critical health issues
- Being introduced by friends to people who become collaborative partners in new business or creative endeavors
- Finally enjoying success with dating after divorce

- Having ideas for a new fiction series come through dreams after a creative drought that had them doubting their ability to continue writing.

When they started working with me, these students and clients didn't imagine that such successes were even possible. We dug up their dreams, worked on developing their goals, and then created steps they could take to ask for help from the guides, watch for signs, and act on the guidance and opportunities that seemed to drop into their laps. You now have the tools that will allow similar surprises to show up in your life.

TRY THIS

As you read or heard me read the list above, what popped in your head? How might you call in support for goals you're already pursuing? How could you ask for help to decide the best course of action if you're undecided about what to do next? Here's an example script:

"I call upon all my guides who can help me break down my goals into actionable steps and be efficient with my energy and time so I can succeed in reaching my goals with ease, grace, flow, and joy. I ask for support in noticing the ways I block my flow, and guidance to joyfully create the success I seek. I'm deeply grateful for the help."

THE GODDESS GUIDE TO GOAL SETTING

I HAVE A GODDESS COUNCIL that includes a variety of goddesses I can call upon, depending on what's going on. The Goddess

Isis is one of my main guides, and she is always present when I'm trying to create something.

Here's how I like to explain working with the goddesses: Archangel Michael is the sky, vast and powerful. The Goddess Isis folds the sky into a laser and asks what you want to do with it. Goddesses bring the power of that laser to your goal. They help me target what I want and where I want to go, and they come in full-on with how to get it done.

The goddesses gave me a concise framework for completing goals with their support: envision, empower, anchor, and act. Here's how it works for me:

Envision. This is the dreaming part, using your imagination in as much detail as you can. How does this goal look when it is complete, and how will you feel? What is the specific outcome you're looking for? Imagine as many of the sensory details as possible, especially related to how you'll feel when you've reached your goal. The specific details can and probably will change as you pursue it, but it's the feeling, the resonance of that realized goal that you're aiming for.

Empower. Call in your guides, all the support you need. This isn't a one-and-done request, but it's the next step because it allows you to start and continue to pursue your goals in partnership with them and their energy, power, and wisdom.

Anchor. This is your intention. You anchor yourself to the earth and then anchor your intention to go after and complete your goal. It's important to get grounded and state your goal out loud. If it helps, you can stand up and assume a Wonder

Woman pose (hands on hips, confidently declaring what you intend to do).

Act. This is the step of applying your energy to take inspired action, and it can trip us up because we struggle to understand what is inspired versus what we think we should do. So, ask for help identifying your next *inspired* action. I always go back to what feels joyful. An action might feel intimidating or like it's a bit too much, but if it makes you feel excited, even gleeful, that's inspired. Think of how little kids play with complete abandon—we want to bring a similar energy to the pursuit of our dreams and goals.

Tara Mohr, author of the book *Playing Big* and creator of a great program of the same name, talks about two different kinds of fear. The first is the fear we feel when we imagine what could go wrong (often invented and improbable) that makes us shrink away from doing or trying something. We feel the second kind of fear when we're expanding, occupying more space than we're used to. This fear is called *yirah* in Hebrew, and it can feel exciting at the same time. We're aiming for the feeling of *yirah* in our goals and inspired actions. Remember "How good can you let it be?" Links to Tara's book and program are included on the resource page of my website: https://julesapollo.com/extras.)

Again, this isn't a one-and-done kind of process. You might go through it and change some of the details or even your goal after you take action. I'd be surprised if you didn't.

You can do the four steps quickly. After your envisioning stage, you can set up a goals council and call them in, just as you'd set up a meeting at work. How do you do this? You just call them in. If there's a specific being you'd like to have support from, call them in. If you don't have a specific guide you'd like to work with, you can ask for guides related to helping you succeed at completing your goal. Don't worry, there's a script for this shared in the coming paragraphs.

You're not being graded on any of this, and you don't need to tell anyone you use this approach if it feels like you're making it up (and just because something is imagined doesn't mean it isn't real). I called in the energies of Jane Austen, Louisa May Alcott, and Beryl Markham to help me write from my heart and to get this book done. All these writers produced works that I admire and when it wasn't easy for women to get published. Does that mean I think Jane is sitting next to me? No, but I do imagine her sitting in the safari tent I use for writing.

One of the most joyful ways for me to create is in community with my guides. It's playful and empowering at the same time. Who do you want on your goal council? You could start by saying something like:

"I'm calling forth all my guides of highest light who can support me in reaching my goal of (whatever you want, starting a business, for example). Please bring me inspiration and support and help me envision the best possible result I can create, discern what actions I should take and what I can leave to you, and make the process exciting and fun. I call forth the energy of (specific guide or archetypal energy of creative mastery, for instance, if you have someone in mind). Please make your guidance clear and easy to understand. I'm so grateful for the support. Thank you."

Maybe there are sports legends, inventors, politicians, or pirates you always wanted to meet if time travel were a thing.

Figures from mythology or ancient cultures to serve as archetypal guides. You can call them in. If their energy can help you, it doesn't matter whether they are archetypes, mythological figures, or real people. Let it be easy and let it be fun.

HOW I WORK ON GOALS WITH MY GUIDES

I WORK WITH MY GUIDES on specific tasks and big goals related to the planet. We are very much a partnership and a family—one that functions and communicates well, unlike what we sometimes experience with our physical families. I'm pragmatically spiritual; I do what works, and this works for me. It helps me get things done and keep focused on working from my heart instead of letting my lizard brain direct traffic (to the extent that this is possible; checking in on it is part of the process). This is private work that I do with my guides, and I'm only sharing it here to show you a broader picture of what working with your guides might look like.

Here are a couple of examples of how I work with my guides. My energy work with them has the overall goal of creating a thriving, just, and healthy world, so these actions are in support of that broad goal. This is my mission, and the purpose for my embodiment now. (I still ask the guides to help me find a parking space, too).

Anchoring light.

One benefit of all the work I've done to release limiting beliefs is that I'm able to access higher frequencies of light and be in harmonic resonance with my guides. This means that in partnership with my guides, I can anchor love and light both to support the planet in general and to focus on specific places where there is violence or hunger, for instance. We bring in higher energies to anchor love, compassion, and peace and offset or counteract energies such as racism, bigotry, and other types of discrimination.

I use social media to determine areas where I want to focus our energy and work. For instance, I'll spend a few minutes looking at news highlights (and it's generally only a few minutes so I don't get dragged down into despair). Whatever catches my eye with its stupidity, makes my blood boil, or hurts my heart becomes my focus for the day. Then I turn off my computer or put down my phone, call in my guides, and ask for their light and love to join mine as we send love and energy to that situation.

Here's an example: where there are wars, I call in all the guides who work with and through me. I call upon Divine Peace and Divine Justice and ask them to be present. I call upon the angelic hosts to anchor light into the earth to protect innocents from violence. I anchor the energies of Divine Oneness into the soil, water, and air, into the political entities involved, into the hearts of the troops, and into social media networks and news outlets around the globe covering this issue so that people's hearts and energies are also focused on peace.

I call upon the light to be anchored and unceasingly renewed until peace is present. I ask what inspired actions I can take on the physical plane to support peace and protect innocents and the earth from violence and destruction. I hold an image of peace, of calm stillness, and of the miracles of wonder and grace to bless everyone involved and bring them in line with the divine plan for a peaceful planet.

Does this change the world? Not completely, but it helps. Just because I can't stop a war by meditating on it doesn't mean it isn't part of my responsibility as an embodied soul to send light where I can, to call in all the support I can, and to then act on the physical plane to help make things better.

Are there organizations working for peace or delivering aid that I can support with funds or by sharing their work? Yes. Are there letters I can write and other physical actions I can take? Yes. And I do these things. But I also feel it's my responsibility to do the energy work that I can, pull in all the power and love that I have access to through my guides, and apply it every time I notice the world needs it. The world needs *all* our light now. I can act on the physical plane and keep doing the energy work as well.

Earth work.

This is what I call my work in support of the planet and moving humanity toward living in closer harmony with nature. I'm trained as a forester and worked in the environmental field for more than thirty-five years. I've learned detailed, technical knowledge about ecological systems and the environment that I apply in specific work with my guides to anchor light into the planet and energetically support ecosystems that are under threat.

Many people want to help the planet. One way is to use the light of our guides and souls to anchor light into Earth. For example, as part of my morning energy work, I call upon my guides and anchor all the light we are into the planet in support of vibrant ecosystems and a balanced way of life. I do this for Earth as a whole and for specific areas of concern such as the Okavango Delta in Botswana, an unspoiled area of vibrant beauty and importance for a wide array of animals, plants, wetlands, and ecosystems. I act in the physical world as well, but I start from the energetic space and move outward as inspired.

A lot of my specific focus on nature comes from what catches my eye in the news. For example, if there is a threat to an area of critical biodiversity from the actions of oil and gas companies, I call upon all my guides, nature spirits, and star beings to protect the area and to anchor light that can block and transmute harmful actions. I can then sign petitions against disruptive activities, support businesses in the area that protect the landscape, donate to ecological or social organizations, and share information and comment about it on social media—all as feels appropriate and inspired.

I also sense the presence of energy grids around the planet that impact how we act as humans. There's a long history of a powerful few using energy grids and societal norms to keep much of the population subservient and to trigger anger and violence in people. I work with my guides to anchor energies of Divine Oneness into triangulation networks that can alter that contamination (I told you we get technical). We also work to override frequencies set up to trigger racist violence and replace them with creation codes for a just, new way of being human on the planet.

There's a lot that can be done energetically to help the planet. The same is true of impacts to the oceans, or to Indigenous communities. That might seem unlikely given the level of abuse to natural systems and the violent history of colonization around the planet. But I refuse to accept that we are helpless to create a balanced world, so I use my knowledge and connections to a vast array of spiritual support to apply my intentions, imagination, and energy toward creating a new Earth and a new way of being human in support of nature, peace, and justice.

Is there a similar cause that always gets you riled up when you read about it in the news? Use your energy, time, and the support of your guides to change it. That's part of the reason you're here right now.

Does this mean I never feel despair? Not at all. I frequently do, it's an emotional state I've sunk into many times. So what do I do? I ask for comfort first, then I ask for clarity on next steps, and support to make as big an impact as I can. There are many many beings of light around the planet now, providing energy and innovative ideas at this time of the collapse of old power systems. Use your particular skills and interests to call in guides that can help you make an impact as well. Creating a healthy, just, peaceful planet is going to take all of us.

TRY THIS

If reading about how I work with my guides makes you wonder how you could do similar work, ask them.

What skills do you have that could be applied to create a more just world and healthy planet? What brings you great joy that you could use, in work with your guides, to anchor more light and spread more love around? Do you have technical expertise that could be applied in partnership with your guides to create a better world?

Everything helps, and all your love is needed now. It's time to play with the light that you and your guides bring. Just moving through your day surrounded by the love you've called in, with an open heart, helps a great deal and keeps your energy high.

After all this talk about dreams, goals, and the tools you can use to work with your guides, I hope you feel ready to dive into the deep end and create a practice that fits your life. Great timing, as that's just what we'll do in Chapter 6.

CHAPTER 6
CREATING YOUR PRACTICE

Louisiana, 2006. The move to Louisiana has been a huge cultural shock for my sons, coming from a Chicago suburb to a town with no stoplights, not to mention different weather, accents, manners, and food.

Not long after we arrive, one of the kids comes home after visiting a schoolmate's home and says, in shock, "Mom, they don't have any books in their house." In our home, we have bookshelves in almost every room. My kids' schools, while good for the area, are almost a year behind what they were studying in Illinois.

I ignored what I knew from my own childhood would be a rough transition for the kids. I'm naively ill-equipped for office politics and find that sweet Southern manners can hide well-sharpened teeth lunging after the available advancement opportunities. And my finances are a wreck—our house in Illinois hasn't yet sold because the housing market fell there just as I bought in Louisiana at the height of the post-Katrina boom.

This is another notch in my belt of self-sabotage: deciding (with my mind) what I want to do instead of checking in with my heart and guidance, then pushing and shoving my way into the situation instead of finding ways to make it easy. I've become better at asking for help from my guides, but I'm still stubbornly clinging to my beliefs about how most things should get done. I feel like I'm fighting against life because I'm fatally flawed—like maybe there's something inherently wrong with me that pushes away good things.

Of course, it's not all bad: the kids adapt, and it's in this home, looking out over a small pond at sunset each night, that I go deep into my connection with my guides and start rooting around in the deeply buried beliefs that keep tripping me up.

I got a mosquito bite while I was in the Peace Corps that turned into a staph infection on my leg, and the doctor had to dig around to get rid of the dead bits before it could start to heal. That's what my work with my guides became for the next decade after we moved to Louisiana: healing the staph infection of my low self-worth. It was just as smelly and messy as you might imagine.

And it was a missed opportunity, because I could also have been asking for help to make my life better. I did learn this over time, but I could have been getting support from the start with things like my health. Paying attention to the help my guides put in my path but that I ignored, like tapping into my younger brother's financial wizardry to manage my money. Although I frequently felt joy and happiness, I missed out on asking for ease.

That's why I'm breaking everything down into easy steps for you: so you'll be able to take full advantage of the guidance you can get when you simply ask for help. So you can start from the beginning with a framework for moving forward with ease and joy, and so you can create a life that's as good as you'll allow it to get.

The point of this chapter is to pull together the pieces we've already discussed and create a quick template, with scripts, for your practice that you can adjust over time.

We're going to set up a practice that fits into your life so you have a better chance of doing it. The most important part is to make it easy. There are a few things you can do to approach your practice that way from the start.

Figure out the best time of day for you to work with your guides. Choose a time when you'll be able to focus on the process. There's no sense trying to work with them right before you go to sleep if you're always exhausted. What time of day are you most alert and efficient? Squeeze in a few minutes during that period to reach out to your guides.

Stay open to being guided, moved, or inspired. I read once that Oprah asks to be blessed into service each day—that's another way to look at being moved or inspired.

Be open to answers or what you're looking for coming in unanticipated ways. If you ask about money, be open to it coming to you through the mail, from a friend, or just showing up in your bank account. You might find it on the ground, win it as a prize, or earn it through getting new clients. You might receive an unexpected raise or bonus, or perhaps a refund will show up. You might be paid for old work or get a call out of the blue to help someone who can pay you. Guidance sometimes comes in roundabout ways that may not at first look like you're getting what you want.

You don't need to speak about all these possibilities, but you can ask for what you request to show up easily and joyfully and then let it go, trusting that your prayers and requests are heard.

Trusting the process means several things:

- Trusting your guides are around and that they will help you
- Trusting that your requests are heard and will be acted upon
- Trusting yourself to understand the guidance you receive
- Trusting yourself to take the actions you're inspired to take

You can ask your guides to help you trust. You can ask them to help you understand the guidance you get. And you can keep asking for clarity and comfort to be part of all your interactions with your guides. Being able to trust the guides and yourself is a huge part of working with them, so note anywhere you feel resistance or doubt when you read or hear the list above. Making requests for what you want and adding "or something better" can help you surrender to the way your request shows up.

I want to share a positive follow-up to the opening of this chapter to emphasize the benefits of even a sporadic practice: by the time 2011 rolled around, I'd been working with the guides, entraining to their energies, releasing outdated patterns, expanding the group of guides I worked with, and refining my channeling to the point that I began writing a weekly blog about my meditation adventures, teaching others how to get started, and channeling meditations to include in my courses.

It didn't feel like great progress while I was in the middle of it, but when I looked back as part of documenting my practices, it was very clear to me that partnering with my guides to reach my dreams and goals had made exponential improvements to many parts of my life.

With that in mind, let's frame out a practice for you.

SETTING EXPECTATIONS

IT'S USUAL TO FEEL A bit nervous and insecure when you think about starting to reach out to your guides: "Will I do it right? Do I really have guides? Will they want to work with me? Have I made any mistakes in my life so bad that they won't work with me?"

Let's be clear on all of these: there's no wrong way to do this, you have many guides, and they will always work with you, no matter what. But it can take a while for you to start sensing them—or just to trust that they are with you whether you sense anything or not. Partly it's them figuring out how to communicate with you in ways you'll notice. This is why I keep mentioning that guidance can be subtle. Just note what comes up in both your internal and external lives.

Even though your guides are with you, you won't necessarily sense their physical presence. In fact, most of us don't. I seldom sense my guides. Did you just glide over that sentence? I don't often feel my guides around me. I just know they're there and trust that they will help whenever I ask them to. This confidence comes from decades of them showing me that this is true, even though I ran away from their guidance many times because I didn't believe it could be that easy. For a long time, I believed that life was hard, so I didn't trust that something was true if it was easy. They had their work cut out for them, teaching me what I'm sharing with you.

I most often feel my guides around—through goose bumps, usually—when I'm talking with someone and the guides want me to share something with that person. The difference between when I started and how I interact with them now is that I know that they are there and I trust them (and myself), so I don't ask for verification; I just ask for help and then expect it to come.

If you can start your practice letting it feel natural (like you assume the lights will turn on when you flip a switch), resting in the assurance that you have loving support ready to help, and suspending any need to define how you get that support, you'll find the process more joyful, surprising, and comforting.

SCRIPTS TO HELP YOU BEGIN

HERE ARE SOME SCRIPTS TO help you get started. You can use these words to start and then revise them to fit you and your guides over time. The point is to just begin. Imagine me right next to you, holding a space for you to feel ready to create your own approach to working with your guides. All of this is flexible and meant to support, not inhibit, you. Here are the scripts, broken into the steps of beginning, request, clarity, and gratitude.

Beginning.

- "I set the intention that I am in a safe space while I talk with my guides, and I invoke the presence and protection of my guides of highest love to create that safe space."
- "I intend to be grounded and centered, with a still, calm mind, so I may best perceive the presence of my guides and the information they have to share with me."
- "I intend to work with only those guides of highest light and love, and I call forth all my guides who meet those criteria to support me now."

Request.

- "I ask that the guidance I receive be clear and easily understood. I ask for support in understanding the guidance and having clarity on the next steps and actions that best support my highest and best good now."
- Use what applies in the following list or something similar to ask for what you need.
  - "I'm asking for help with..."
  - "I'd like to get guidance related to..."
  - "I'm asking for a clear sign that you are with me."
  - "Please bring me inspiration and clarity on next steps, I'd love to create..."
  - "Please give me strength and commitment to reach my goal, I've felt like stopping..."
  - "I have a big dream; please help me hold a clear vision of how to make this come true..."

Clarity.

- "Can you share more details about this?"
- "Am I perceiving correctly? Please help me clearly understand."
- "I'd love to receive guidance and support on how to start making something happen."

Gratitude

- "I trust that the guidance I am getting, either now or in the future in response to this request, is in support of my intention and for my highest good. Thank you all. I'm grateful. So be it and so it is."

TRY THIS

Play with these steps and scripts—make them your own. All of this can be changed. It's great when it works and flows all in and around you. If you don't sense anything immediately after you make your request, go on with your day and come back later.

FROM THE GUIDES

Focus on the new and release the old. Ask for our help, protection, and guidance during your days and rest. Say, "I call upon the assistance, protection, and guidance of the archangelic hosts to be ever with me through this day and night. Light my path, clear my way." We are ever near and are all about you now. Bring us closer to your heart. The strength of our love, its fierce and powerful grace, will astound you.

QUIETING INNER CRITICS

MY INNER CRITICS' FAVORITE TOOL is a rapier wit designed to cut me down to size: "Who do you think you are? You have nothing to say that's worth listening to. You've got to be kidding if you think you can write." (Accompanied by cackling.) Or: "Just wait until they see the rot inside you—they'll run away like everyone else." They'll wake me up in the middle of the night in a panic about some mistake I made a decade ago as a mother, making it seem so bad it's like a fatal error in a program and like my life should just crash down around me and burn.

Does any of this sound familiar to you? If so, your inner critics might be digging in here. In fact, you may have skimmed over the sample scripts above and decided that you're not ready and will keep reading or listening and come back to this later. That's ok, but if it's your lizard brain jumping in, please know it's normal and there are ways to let go of things that restrict you. The key to lowering the volume of the inner critics is to lean into the support you can call on from your guides as you face the critics, question their logic, and act to release their hold on your mind and energy.

It's good to have fears and doubts come up because then you can release them with the help of your guides. This is something that might happen a lot, no matter how long you work with your guides. Any time we try to change or move into greater freedom, the inner critics marshal the troops and come calling. This happens both when we start something and as we progress. Releasing old concepts of self will always be part of your practice, so you may as well have a process in place to make it easier.

Your guides come to you in wisdom, surrounded by light and love and bathing you in these higher frequencies. Any lower-frequency energies, outdated patterns, or limiting beliefs you have will come to your attention as you work with the guides because the old energies are not in resonance with the energy you're calling forth to help you.

It's all physics: People and ideas feel good to us when they resonate with us—when they have the same vibe, you might say. As you work with your guides, you'll get comfortable with their higher frequencies. And each time you interact with them, you raise your frequency a bit to get closer to theirs. This is the concept of harmonic resonance.

It's not necessary to know the history of a pattern or revisit it to resolve it. It's not helpful to get into the energy of a pattern if it came from an abusive or damaging incident, or if it's an old family pattern. The point is to let it go. This is another place where your imagination, or a brief ritual, comes in handy.

Here are some things you could do to release old stuff as it comes up. See what works for you.

- Write old patterns down on a piece of paper and burn it. This can be a fun ritual to do with the moon cycles. I tend to let go of old things with the full moon and welcome new patterns or desires with the new moon. Howling is optional but freeing.
- Take a ritual bath to release an old pattern. Imagine it draining away with the water.
- Set an intention to be free of whatever's holding you back and imagine yourself in a shower of light—light that flows like water, and the old pattern is mud on your skin. Stand in this shower until the water at your feet looks clear. This is what I do at the beginning of each session with my guides in my inner sanctuary.
- Write down what your inner critics say and read it out loud. Is it logical? Would you say it to a friend? If not, tell

that pattern you're no longer interested in hearing illogical thoughts and if it wants to participate in your life, it needs to be helpful or be quiet—and get your guides to support you in this. For me, this isn't a one-and-done deal, but something I use consistently. Over time, it has shut up the worst of my inner demons.

- Imagine a big bonfire and your ancestor spirits dancing around it to support you. Add some drumming or music, light some incense, and see the scene as vividly as possible as you imagine burning up whatever stinky thinking has held you back by throwing it in the fire or standing in the middle of the flames to burn it away. I stand in the flames for old family stuff.

- See each pattern like the skin of a snake and shed it if it's an old identity that no longer fits ("I don't have anything of value to share" is one I had). I imagine it as an entire skin, like a full-body mask, yank it off, and into the fire it goes.

- Plan any or all of this as part of a full moon or year-end ritual, throw in a tarot reading for the new year or cycle, and have a party with your guides. Might as well power up as part of your ritual of release. I share my favorite tarot and oracle decks here: https://julesapollo.com/extras.

TRY THIS

Pick one of these suggestions or create something that works for you in a similar way and use it on your inner critics' favorite intrusion into your day. Keep these suggestions handy for the next time you're ready to release an old pattern.

HOW TO FIND TIME TO TALK
TO YOUR GUIDES

You may have skimmed past this whole chapter, thinking that you have no time to try any of this. You may be thinking that this is all fine and good for me, as I seem to have time to talk to my guides all the time, but you don't.

I created all the tips and scripts I'm sharing with you when I was a single parent and had no breaks from being with my kids. I had a long commute, unending housework, a more-than-full-time job, and three sons who deserved my time and attention. I used the tips below to free up a few more minutes here and there throughout the day so I wasn't so exhausted, or to end my day (and work) earlier so I could work for a few minutes with my guides and meditate before bed.

The following simple things worked for me to grab some extra time in the day. See which of these you could apply to your day.

- Do a quick check-in with your guides while your coffee is brewing.
- Run through a quick visualization or journal for a few minutes while the kids do their homework (see Chapter 5 for a reminder of how to use these tools to go after your goals with your guides).
- Leave the dishes to soak until tomorrow and call in your guides instead—or talk to them while you're doing dishes or loading the dishwasher. I find warm water soothing, so this is a good way for me to relax my mind and open my heart to guidance.

- Delegate or outsource something you hate. This can involve finding software to help with a task or making something you do regularly more efficient, like ordering groceries online and doing curbside pickup instead of shopping in the store. Then use the freed-up time to focus on your dreams.
- If you're waiting for a meeting to start, do some deep breathing so your mind and body aren't restricting your flow of inspiration.
- Turn off the computer early and spend that saved time to focus on goals.
- Run through the details of your goal with your guides while you're folding laundry or cooking. Cleaning is a great general way to ask your guides questions and allow answers to come while your body is doing the work.
- Figure out the times of day when you're most efficient and make working with your guides your priority at those times. Conversely, do things that can be completed without intense energy commitments during times when your energy or focus lag: for me, those things are laundry, dishes, and walking the dog. My energy tends to have revived at the end of these activities, so I get a double benefit: things are done, and I have improved focus to boot.
- Grab a few minutes before sleep to check in with your guides for inspired actions to take the next day.
- Keep a notebook by your bed and take the first ten minutes in the morning to write before anyone knows you're awake. If I wake up remembering a dream, I try and figure out what its message might be.

You need to decide that you can and will find the time you want. This is where you commit to honoring your creativity and passion. Decide that you will find a way, no matter what your family needs or what work deadlines you have, to feed your soul and free your heart by creating what wants to come out into the world.

I found the superpower of intention when my kids were tiny and I felt like I was dissolving, like salt in water, under the weight of all the work with no time for rest, let alone creative flow to sustain me. I had to find a way, so I intended to find a way, and I did (in many tiny ways). Make a note on your phone or put a sticky note on your mirror as a reminder to take this time for yourself.

Once you reap the benefits of a few minutes, it will be easy to find more. Think of it as a scavenger hunt. Most of these suggestions are just about using your time intentionally: what do you want to get out of your days and weeks? Make that the focus of the minutes you're grabbing.

TRY THIS

From what's been discussed in this chapter, what pops in your head to try? Pick two things and try them out today. How did that work? Note your progress and keep going.

CHECK-IN

WE WENT THROUGH A LOT in this chapter. You might need to let it settle for a bit before things begin to fall into place and you see how it can fit into your life. Don't forget to be playful with it and experiment. It's not meant to be serious or overwhelming. The point of all this is to feel better about being able to get answers and support when you need it.

Let's do another quick check-in like we did at the beginning of the book: Using a range of one to five, with one being the lowest and five being the highest, answer these questions:

- Do you know how to work with your guides?
- Do you know what guidance looks like and how to tell if you're getting it?
- Do you feel confident that you can tell the difference between guidance and just making something up?

Make a quick note of your numbers for each question to compare with your results from the beginning of the book. How do your numbers compare to the first check-in? Look at all the new approaches you've learned and scripts you have. You've made great progress.

Let's revisit the vision you created in Chapter 1 of how you'll feel once you're able to work with your guides and trust the answers you're getting: calm, confident, clear, and creating what you want. Take a few minutes to truly see, smell, hear, feel, and imagine this as real. Is it easier to imagine this state of being now? How has your vision changed since you started the book? Do you feel more confident? Can you see it more clearly?

If creating an initial process to work with your guides isn't falling easily into place, the approaches in the next chapter might work. We all need help to quiet our minds so we can easily sense the guidance that's already around and being shared with us.

And there are many ways to make this process work for you, no matter how chaotic your life is. I feel that the chaos in the world will only keep increasing, at least for a bit, so having ways to feel peaceful for a few minutes as you go about your day is gold. Keep going to find out how.

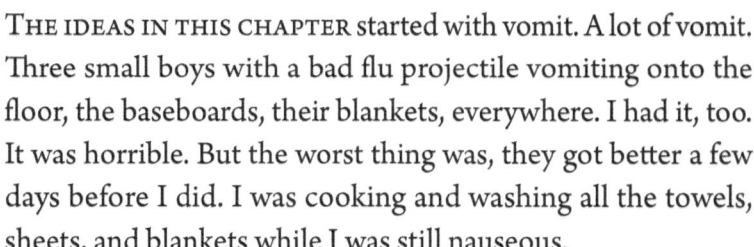

CHAPTER 7
HOW TO QUIET YOUR MIND
IN TIMES OF CHAOS

THE IDEAS IN THIS CHAPTER started with vomit. A lot of vomit. Three small boys with a bad flu projectile vomiting onto the floor, the baseboards, their blankets, everywhere. I had it, too. It was horrible. But the worst thing was, they got better a few days before I did. I was cooking and washing all the towels, sheets, and blankets while I was still nauseous.

We'd just come back from a road trip to my mom's house. It was winter and the heat was out in my car, so everyone was covered up with blankets and… you guessed it. They started throwing up a hundred miles from home and the last twenty miles were ugly. To top it off, I had a huge cold sore under my nose and had to go into a gas station to pay, and I'm sure I smelled like vomit by that point.

I came out of that experience knowing I had to find ways to release tension every day and pay attention to my body so I could survive being a single parent. I didn't get child support or have days without the kids, and I had no family nearby. I was exhausted, depleted, and depressed.

I knew I had to find ways to recharge and relax so I'd sleep well once I finally got to bed, instead of waking up in a panic in the middle of the night. And I wanted to feel joyful at the end of each day, that feeling of bobbing along the surface instead of being pulled under. Slogging along never works for me; I have to find a way to feel better so I can keep going. The steps I share in this chapter are how I did that.

Parenting in general is tough and time-consuming. It's hard even if you're a parent with adequate funds and support. If you're a caregiver for your parents or other adults and feel financial stress, or lack support or adequate time for yourself, the suggestions that follow can help. If you don't have kids but have a demanding career, I'm sure you too can benefit from ways to relax more throughout your day. Given how chaotic life can feel, these suggestions can probably help anyone who's feeling tense. We have to find ways to feel calm, even as we handle all of the day-to-day needs and crises, or we'll never perceive the guidance we're getting.

When you're stressed and exhausted, you won't pick up on subtle nudges and you struggle to find even a few minutes to focus on guidance. In this chapter, we'll go over how to calm your mind no matter what's going on around you.

HOW TO TELL IT IT'S GUIDANCE OR YOUR MIND

I WORRIED ABOUT THIS A lot when I started as I thought I might be making things up. This is a frequent concern of my students too. It's actually easy: your guides are never mean, insulting, or cross with you. The feelings they radiate are expansive, joyful, supportive, and/or comforting. While your inner critics can sometimes seem quiet, they generally tell you to do what keeps you contained and small. Listening to their critical voices can make you feel bad or lack the confidence to make big changes.

I used to double-check that I was hearing correctly, and you might want to do this as you begin to sense guidance. One way to do this is to use muscle testing, also referred to as applied kinesiology: I press the pads of my left forefinger and thumb together, then try to push the fingers apart with the same fingers of my right hand in response to a question and see if I meet resistance or not. I'm no expert at explaining this—there is plenty of information online, though, so search for a video that will show you how to do it (I tried to film one, but I have short, fat fingers so it's hard to see what I'm doing and then I kept laughing because it looked so silly). I also use tarot cards to ask questions. The main thing I still do when I'm really tense and unsure that I'm hearing correctly is stop asking, move around a bit (get a glass of water or stretch), and then ask again after making sure I'm grounded and in a safe space.

Your spirit guides are positive, and it feels good to work with them. If the guidance you receive makes you doubt yourself or feel fearful or frantic about missing out, that's either your inner critics talking, or you are making decisions solely from your mind and disconnected from your inner wisdom.

I've invested in many courses and programs—on how to start a business, how to write books, how to be a successful author, how to make a living from my dreams, how to make more money, how to be more productive, how to be more confident—out of a fear of missing out and the feeling that

I wasn't good enough. I used to feel I had to grab at whatever might make me better and more acceptable so I could avoid rejection.

I make a point now of checking in with guidance before I invest. I also know what truth feels like in my body—what a positive opportunity feels like, even if it makes me stretch a bit—versus the feeling that I'm not good enough and am trying to find a course or coach to help me feel like I'm a better person. Do you know the difference between guidance you trust and your inner critics? Do you have ways to check? Start with the suggestions above and see what works for you.

TRY THIS

Take a moment right now and think of some of your standard inner criticism. Imagine someone standing in front of you and saying these things to you or hearing someone say them to a friend or family member. They're like rude posts on social media. It's easier to see how silly they are if you expose them to the light of logic. You've outgrown them now and so you and they are ready for healing love.

Some of my inner critics are old Midwestern farm wives, like my grandmothers and great-grandmothers. "Get your work done or no play" and "You're getting too big for your britches" kind of voices. Judging and shaming are two of their favorite games. It can help to give your inner critics names or to imagine them in detail. It's easier to shut them up that way.

Here are some of the ways I've used to quiet them. My approach varies based on the voices and how nasty or debilitating they are.

- I imagine the mean grandmas on a big front porch with rockers and sweet tea, maybe some knitting. I often see them fall asleep. They didn't know times of rest, so this is a gift I can give them.

- For others who want to constrain my exuberance, who judge and shame, I take a different approach. This is one I really like: I imagine I'm at the head of a big table in an office boardroom. (Make it as fancy and sterile as you wish, that can help.) Mine is always sleek, expensive, and in a high-rise in downtown Chicago. Acting as the CEO of my life, I call the voices to the table and ask for updates. They start up their usual tripe; I stop them and say that's old news, we've already resolved that—do you have anything new? And since most of these voices are one-trick ponies, complaining about the same thing over and over, they just look down sheepishly. I tell them that they only get to keep their seat at the table if they bring something helpful and constructive.

- I get into old loops of self-criticism. These days, I just tell those voices that it's not true what they're saying and I'm not going to listen to it. I find that some resolute firmness does the trick. I don't deserve to be treated to such tirades and neither do you.

- My main way to quiet them is to go into my inner sanctuary. There's an old, thick, medieval-looking wooden door to get into that space. I go inside and shut the door, and this keeps out everything that isn't for my highest good.

- Sometimes I surprise them by giving them a big hug, asking that they be surrounded in love. I'm usually not patient enough to do this, but it's a surefire way to silence them for a good amount of time. My most fearful critics are the ones that respond best to this. I wrap them in a bear hug, and they calm right down, like a frightened child (which the fears really are).

This is where your imagination comes in. What technique might you use? Once you clearly hear what the inner critics are saying, an easy question to ask is if you'd say what you're hearing to a friend. If it isn't representative of the way you'd talk with someone you care about, it isn't something you need to tolerate creeping into your day and your energy.

It doesn't matter what you do to shut them up so long as you realize that these voices aren't speaking the truth, and you can move past them to get what you want. Progress comes when you keep going instead of getting stuck in their nonsense.

HOW TO QUICKLY FEEL CALMER

THE FOLLOWING SUGGESTIONS DON'T TAKE any time. You can do them as you go about your regular day. They just require some shifts: shifts in focus, in believing what you can do, in how you manage time and energy, and how you take care of yourself.

As you choose to put these practices in place, you'll move from feeling overwhelmed, discouraged, exhausted, and unappreciated at times to feeling consistently calm, relaxed, and confident that you can handle whatever life throws at you.

I've included brief breaks that take little to no time and are meant to help sustain your energy, lift your mood, or save you time. These can be sprinkled throughout your day, with the intent to help you get to the end of it feeling less stress and more energy. That way, you can squeeze in work with your guides when you have a few minutes.

I also listed some ideas for renewal rituals: ways to treat yourself once a week or so that are focused on your senses, creativity, or deep rest.

What's the result of taking these small steps? They provide fuel and sustenance so you can deal with daily life and still have time and energy to create what you want.

As you read through the list below, you'll recognize things that you're already doing, things that you already do well, and others that you can adapt to fit into your day or week right now to make things easier. Looking for solutions to what's bugging you is proactively making change, which is one of the reasons you found this book.

I came up with these simple things to let go of stress when I was freaking out so I could make better decisions and be the mom my kids needed. These tips also work to help with career-related fears, time crunches, steep learning curves, competing demands, and financial strain.

The most important one is the first: taking three deep breaths changes your body from anxious to serene, at least for a bit. Do more deep breathing if you need to—I usually do three sets of three.

If you try nothing else, do the breathing. It can really help, and you can do it no matter what else is going on. Can't pay a bill and are panicking? Take three deep breaths. Feeling exhausted but the kids are sick? Take three deep breaths. Frozen with anxiety about the future? Three big ones and then two more sets. I sigh loudly when I breathe out if I'm worried; it seems to release the tension. This breathing practice strengthens your lungs and gets more oxygen to your body, so it's great for your overall health as well.

Here are my top suggestions for things you can try to feel calmer. Most of them take a few minutes at most.

- Take three deep belly breaths with a big sigh on the exhales.
- Check your body, breathe, and stretch to release tense muscles. Tight muscles tire you out.
- Get outside. Even a five-minute walk can help. Or listen to the sound of rain or birdsong while you work. Even photos or videos of nature can relax you a lot. YouTube videos can be great for this. I love videos of walks in different forests with the sounds of the wind in the trees and birds in the background.
- Listen to a favorite song and have a solo dance party. Music and dancing send happy hormones through the body. Make an emergency playlist for bad days and keep it handy on your phone. This is great for loud singing in the car, too, which is another great way to release tension and feel better.
- Have a good ugly cry in the shower. I used to do this when the kids were small so they wouldn't hear me. When I finally realized how much tension and stress crying releases, I just let myself cry whenever I needed to; I didn't need a specific reason.
- Get and/or give a big, squishy hug from your kids or a dog or stuffed animal. Squishy hugs are the best!
- Close your eyes and imagine your perfect peaceful place, your inner sanctuary—someplace safe, serene, and

beautiful. This is great for a commute if you're on a bus or train. (See Chapter 11 for more on creating your inner sanctuary.)

- Look into the mirror and remind yourself that you're strong, resilient, and will figure it out. Be kind to yourself and be your own cheerleader.

- Give yourself a beauty break. This is similar to the Artist Date described in Julia Cameron's *The Artist's Way*, one of my favorite books. It feeds the creative well with images or experiences. If you're crazy busy, you can squeeze a mini beauty break into your day by looking at images of art, places you want to travel, or beauty in nature on Instagram or Pinterest. Watching a movie or listening to a concert works too. I love going to the symphony or to a museum, and watching old movies is the best.

- Enjoy a relaxation ritual with a long bath, or maybe just sitting in bed with a heating pad and a journal or a good book. Let your mind wander and do nothing on your agenda or to-do list.

- Get comfy: put on pajamas and fuzzy socks, grab some pillows and a favorite treat or glass of wine, and relax.

- Take a creation break: bake, paint, color, garden, write, or build. Creating something taps the power of your mind and heart so new ideas and different perspectives can sneak in. I've found that sloppy coloring is a great way to release frustration.

I use the three deep breaths multiple times throughout the day. I used to do it in meetings if I started to get tense, or I'd go into the bathroom and do a series of six or nine breaths and some simple stretches of my shoulders and neck. It still helps me when I'm tired.

Play is important and is neglected if we're stressed. Coloring, blowing bubbles, laughing, baking, taking bubble baths, giving (and receiving) squishy hugs, having dance parties in your kitchen, just being silly—I could cite plenty of research that shows why we need play, but just try it and feel how tension leaves and inspiration flows in.

TRY THIS

Make some notes in your phone, journal, or little notebook of the things that seem fun or easy from the list above and experiment to see what works for you.

Music is absolutely guaranteed to lift my mood and increase my energy. Put on something that you can move to with abandon or restraint, whatever suits your personality. Even a few minutes helps a lot, and you can do this while driving, unloading the dishwasher, taking out the garbage, or cleaning the bathroom. I'm old-school and created a playlist of favorites that you can find here: https://julesapollo.com/extras. Having an emergency feel-good playlist can help in times of trauma, too.

Find funny videos on YouTube to help you get through a tough day.

What's your favorite kind of play? I love blowing bubbles, always have, so I get out into the garden with my dog and some bubbles if the world feels particularly brutal.

RELEASING OLD FEARS AND PATTERNS

I PROBABLY SPEND HALF OF my time with my guides working to release old patterns. When I first started asking for guidance, I figured I'd need to make a lot of improvements to who I was or how I went through life. That hasn't been the case. It's been much more about letting go of stinky thinking so my true nature can come through.

Figuring out what's holding you back and letting it go is something the guides can really help with, especially since a lot of old fears are subconscious and/or based in old family patterns. Noticing and releasing patterns that no longer serve you will be an ongoing part of working with your guides.

It's best to get professional support if you're dealing with issues related to abuse or long-term trauma, but asking your guides for support and following simple release practices can help as well. Here's a sequence that works for me.

- Ask for help releasing your fears, known and unknown, that are affecting your life right now. If you know of a specific fear, state it, but don't limit it to what you're consciously aware of.
- Ask to be shielded and protected by Archangel Michael to keep you safe. You can ask for this generally or specifically (while you are driving or traveling, for instance). This helps keep your energy field clear and prevents you from picking up negative energies floating around other people.
- Ask for help to understand the issue and ways you can move beyond it.

- Ask for help to feel stronger, to know you're capable of releasing and moving past these fears, to feel confident, and to feel the comfort of your guides.
- Ask for help to know that you're okay just as you are, that you're worthy of guidance, love, help, support, and all good things coming to you.
- Ask to be filled with the highest light and love to replace fear, anger, or pain.
- Give thanks for the help.

Here's an easy ritual that many people do with the full moon. Write down what you want to release on a piece of paper or use one small piece of paper for each thing. Burn the paper(s) while imagining the fear floating off you or dropping away like chunks of dirt in the shower. Drink a glass of cool water, intending that the liquid replace your fear with light.

If you find that reading this brings up fears about being able to release your old patterns or get help, add that to the mix. You don't need to relive the fear or go back into the details of what happened to instill the fear, and you don't need to understand how the guides are helping you release it; just let them help you and let it go.

If you have anger instead of fear, you can use the same approach to letting it go. I've had a lot of anger to release over the years.

You might have to do this kind of releasing multiple times for a deep fear or stubborn old belief. I've spent the last decade doing detailed releases of feelings of unworthiness, as they were so deeply buried and came up in different ways after each release. This is normal, so just expect that it might happen. Each time you release the old patterns that restrict you, you fill up with brighter light in line with the energy of your guides. This process is one of the most important parts of gaining confidence and self-acceptance.

Over time, you'll welcome it when fears come up because you know you can release them, and it feels both comforting and empowering to get it done. That's how I feel when I notice another comment from my internal critics: time to let it go and move on with help at hand.

FROM THE GUIDES

We applaud any efforts you make to quiet your mind, as it's so much easier for us to help you when there is stillness within you. We can plant peace and grace in a quiet mind. We can also help you gain this stillness as you struggle with it. Calm eases the entire process; greases it, in a way. Ask us to help with everything and the struggles lessen as progress increases to get you to the point of comfort. When you can perceive our comfort, our interactions are amplified and become joyful. Asking for joyful interactions is a way to bring this in from the beginning.

TRY THIS

What's one old belief or pattern you'd love to be rid of? If you're not sure where to start, think of the most common thing your inner critics say to you and go with that.

Start tackling it using the notes above to help you. If it's a sticky old one like low self-esteem, it'll pop up differently and you might have to go at it in multiple ways; but keep at it using the Whac-A-Mole approach. You'll look back in six months and be amazed at how much calmer you feel.

This work will come in handy in the next chapter as we look at how to get help when life seems to be falling apart around you.

CHAPTER 8
HOW TO GET HELP IN TIMES OF TRAUMA OR TROUBLE

WHEN MY KIDS ARE SIX (twins) and eight, I work about fifteen minutes from home in one of the northern suburbs of Chicago, Illinois. One day they're recovering from sinus infections and don't feel great, so I let them stay home while I go to the office for an hour. I call home before leaving the office to see if they want me to pick up some fast food. They put in their Happy Meal™ orders and I head out.

Ten minutes later, I get a call from home. I answer and it's a man.

Inside my home.

Answering the phone in my house.

I feel like my head is going to explode and I have a hard time controlling the car—I want to accelerate to light speed and rip the throat out of whoever is in my house with my kids.

"Who is this?" I ask, trying not to scream. I'm gripping the wheel so hard it hurts.

The man tells me he's a police officer. He's inside my house, so the kids answered the door and must be so frightened. The police came in response to a 911 call from one of the kids who said he wanted to change his meal order, didn't know where I was, and was hungry.

I tell the officer I'm ten minutes away, already on my way home, and was picking up meals for each of the kids. They'd had breakfast, of course, and now I'd get them lunch after dealing with this, whatever it was.

It's the longest drive of my life. I'm on a two-lane road and it's hard to pass, I'm behind TWO people driving the twenty miles-per-hour speed limit, and when they finally turn, I'm afraid to speed too much since I'm in a speed trap zone and I don't need that delay on top of everything else.

I drive into my quiet subdivision and pull up to the house. There are two police cars, parked at angles like they sped in with their sirens and lights on. At least the lights are off now.

The police meet me on the steps and won't let me go into the house. The kids are peering out the picture window, obviously frightened. I call out to them that everything's okay.

They ask me questions about how long I've been gone and if I do this a lot. They tell me they've gone through the house and found a fork on the floor (yes, this is part of my mom shame: I'm not a perfect homemaker. I refrain from screaming that they could probably find a whole place setting somewhere on the floor if they poke around a little more). They ask when I last fed the kids, and I tell them the boys had breakfast before I left.

The police tell me that they won't take me in now, but I need to go to the police station and turn myself in.

I finally get into the house and the kids are crying and scared. I make them some lunch and the neighbor across the street (we've recently moved to the neighborhood, and I've said hello but don't know her) comes over and asks what's going on. After she leaves, I take the boys to their after-school daycare and head over to the police station to get booked. I am shaking so much, it's hard to steer. I know now what people mean when they say their legs are shaking so hard that they can barely walk.

I cry so hard while being fingerprinted that my eyes swell shut. The young officer booking me tries to make me feel a little better, asking, "This your first time here?" like we're getting a drink at a bar. At least they don't take the kids away.

Fast forward a few weeks and I'm driving down the road after dropping the kids off at school, running through a constant, rapid "Help me, I don't know what to do, help me," and trying not to cry. My court date is coming up and this could affect my custody of the kids—the most important thing in the world to me. I'm afraid I'll be called out and shamed as a mother and I'm so worried that I can't eat. Believe me, that's never happened before.

BAM—Archangel Michael booms into my brain, so loud that if I wasn't alone, I swear someone else could hear it.

"Do. You. Trust. Me?" he asks.

Well, of course. Obviously. "Yes, I'm sorry, I'm just worried."

He tells me he'll be with me and that it will be fine. I try and trust this, but on my court date, I'm freaking out.

I walk into the courtroom, which has about ten rows of benches split into four sections, all facing the judge's bench. It's like a church of justice. The courtroom is packed and all the rows are full.

My lawyer tells me he's requested that we are called to the bench later in the hope that some of the people will be gone. I'd asked before we came what kind of sentence I might get. He'd said it would hopefully just be community service and a fine, and he anticipated it could be about sixty hours.

So how does a single mom do sixty hours of community service without leaving the kids at home alone? I only have forty hours of vacation left and no sick time (that's all been used up for the kids). I try not to think about that right now; it's just making me panic even more. I can't lose the kids—their dad is unable to take care of them and pretty much abandoned us. The lawyer has said that's not going to happen. I'm trying to calm down and trust.

The judge comes in. As he starts working through the docket of cases, he yells out each set of charges so the entire large, packed courtroom can hear. I'm frozen in fear. Surely he won't do this for everyone.

Oh, yes, he does. The huge public shaming keeps going. This is a nightmare: everyone will know I'm a bad mom. I was afraid to have kids because I thought I'd be a bad mom after the violent childhood I had, but I never imagined it would be proven in court. I'm shaking and feel like I'm going to throw up. What if I fall over when I walk up there? What if I pee on myself before then?

The room is emptying but still about half full when it's my turn to go forward. I brace myself for the judge's bellows. I feel everyone watching me, judging me, wondering what I did wrong, how I'm flawed, why I'm here.

I'm having a hard time breathing; my breath is coming in jerks like it does after a hard cry, which I'm a few seconds away from having in front of everyone.

As I walk up to the bench, I feel Archangel Michael right behind me, like I could lean back into him, and I sense angels lining the walls of the entire room.

The judge is looking down at my file. My lawyer walks up and speaks quietly, mentioning my lack of a record and my Peace Corps service. He'd told me this might get me some points. He's speaking so softly I can hardly hear him.

The judge looks up at me. My lawyer prepared me to expect a few questions from the judge. He starts speaking softly, so quietly I must lean forward to hear him.

He asks my name, and I don't remember what else—only a few yes or no questions. My lawyer whispers back the answers. No one else will have any idea what we're talking about, let alone what I've been charged with. I'm starting to feel some relief, but we're not done yet.

The judge says there's no fine, he's giving me thirty hours of community service—the least amount possible—and he expects never to see me again.

I say yes sir, and my lawyer nods that we're done.

Thirty hours. I can use my vacation time. No one at work needs to know.

I feel Archangel Michael again, right beside me. He has helped and protected me.

A few weeks after court, it's 8:30 on a Sunday night and I've just put the kids to bed. It's warm out, so the screen door is open. I hear a knock. It's a social worker from the Illinois Department of Healthcare and Family Services who has been assigned to the case and needs to see the kids. I say they're in bed and she tells me I need to get them up. They all come downstairs and pile onto the sofa. They look at her, she looks at them, and then she looks at me for a while. No one says anything.

She stands up and says she's closing the case; there's no need for state oversight of the children.

That's the protection of Archangel Michael.

One more time.

I'm assigned a probation officer, a short, round, older woman whose white curls are held close to her head by a hairnet. She tries to get me community service at a hospital, but they reject me because of the kind of charges I had. She asks if I'd be interested in working at a seminary. "At least they shouldn't reject me, that wouldn't be very Christian," I say, and we both giggle. She feels so warm and comforting, I'm waiting for her to offer me some home-baked cookies. It's the last time I see her.

I take my week of vacation and head to the seminary, where statues of Archangels Michael and Gabriel line the hall. I wash dishes, drink coffee, and am encouraged to take breaks to pray. There's a jewel-box chapel to Mother Mary, who comes to me in a pink cloud of gentle love whenever I'm there. It's like a spiritual retreat. No one understands why I'm here. One of the young women I'm working with has more than 500 hours of service to complete for traffic-related charges, and the others have to do at least 240 hours.

That's the protection of Archangel Michael.

The booming happened one more time when one of my kids was in legal trouble. This time he came in and said loudly, "Did I not help you?" in the same way. I knew to stop worrying and that everything would be okay even though I couldn't see how. And it was.

It can be most difficult to understand that you have help and guides around you when things are going terribly wrong, and you need help right now. The guides are still there, and simple steps can help you get relief right away so you can keep going. It's particularly difficult to sense guidance when you're tense, but that's when you need it most. It helps to have some emergency actions lined up in advance to help you calm down enough to sense guidance or options; you don't want to try to figure it out when you're panicking.

TIPS TO HELP RIGHT NOW

THESE ARE TIPS FOR WHAT to do in an emergency when you can't breathe but need to keep going. Someone you love is sick, you're in financial distress, you're in a place where you don't feel safe, you don't know how to go on: that's when these suggestions will help.

The intention is to get you through the next few minutes so you can calm down enough to ask for help and for you to feel just a bit better right now. Then you can sense the support you're getting and see options or opportunities that you couldn't when you were so tense.

I've also included tips on how to ask for help for others, and how to ask for forgiveness (for others and yourself), since these can be part of dealing with troubles or trauma.

Again, my number one quick fix that you can do anywhere is to take three deep breaths. Not just any breaths, big belly breaths. Tilt back your head, fill up your gut, hold it for a second, breathe out through your mouth, and wait for a second before you inhale again. Do this three times. For me, it's the short pauses after breathing in and out that do the trick and help me get into a rhythm. If you don't feel any relief from this, take three more deep breaths (I do three sets of three and I always feel better). Is this easy? Yes. Free? Yes. Can you easily fit it into your day? Yes. You can even do it right now, as you read or listen. It's the perfect tip!

Research shows the many benefits of deep breathing. I don't want this to turn into a scientific journal article; you can search online and find thousands of links. But for now, I want you to know it strengthens your lungs, lowers your blood pressure, calms your mind, and gets more oxygen to your brain. I keep mentioning this exercise because it works immediately no matter where you are. Check out the book *Breath* by James Nestor and the author's website for more breathing approaches that might be perfect for you.

Here's a list of other emergency relief measures that my students and I have used to feel a little better right away. If there's a repeat from earlier in the book, it's because it works here too.

- Call in your guides of highest light and those who can provide emergency support. Say, "I call upon all my guides of highest light. I call upon the support of the archangels and all my guides to help me with (whatever you need: safety for your family, miraculous healing, protection, etc.) right now."
- If you don't even know what to ask for, just say (out loud, if possible), "Help me, I don't know what to do," over and over for a few minutes if you need to. I've done this plenty of times while crying on my knees in my closet when I had no idea what to do, but didn't want the kids to hear me.
- Do a quick tension release: cry, stretch, rock, and calm your body as you can. You can do this in the bathroom at work or in a hospital if you need to be discreet.

- Tell the guides that you're tense and need their help to be easily understood, immediate, and ongoing. Tell them you need them to be right next to you as you're too stressed to sense them. This is what I do if my kids are in trouble.
- If you're inspired to do something supportive to help whoever is having an emergency, do it. If you're not sensing guidance, do something mildly physical (I clean or fold laundry; a stretch helps too) to release some tension and give yourself a chance to sense any support or guidance that's coming.
- If nothing comes, keep calling in help and carry on. There's no problem with continuing to repeat a request until you get some relief.
- I ask myself what I can do to feel a little better right now and do it. Sometimes it's just putting on comfy socks and zoning out. Even feeling a tiny bit better helps. It's better than freaking out or feeling so angry I might blow a blood vessel.
- Get and give some hugs. Do you have a stuffed animal? A young child or pet? Squishy hugs are one of the key things that gets me through tough times.
- Stay hydrated. It's amazing how mild dehydration tires you out and affects your mood. It's easy to forget to drink and eat when you're stressed out or going through a family emergency. The last thing you need is a urinary tract infection on top of everything else.
- Give yourself a small break in whatever way you can: let the house be messy, get takeout, take an extra-long shower, have an ugly cry.

- Go into your car, a closet, or anywhere you have some privacy and let out a good scream, then carry on. Howling at the moon is great, too.
- Let help in and be open to miracles showing up (money, comfort, time, energy, healing, inspiration, etc.). Be open to help coming from other people in unexpected ways.
- Laugh. I have a collection of short videos that I go back to a lot whenever I need a quick laugh. This always helps me feel better.
- Did you create a playlist earlier? You can use that now, too. It's good to build one with a range of songs or create different playlists for different moods. When I'm tense, I need different tunes than I do when I'm tired.

The point of all this is to help you feel just a bit better. It's hard to have a clear head when you feel panic or despair, so do whatever you can to rise above that, even for a few minutes at a time. If you can feel a bit calmer, you'll be able to see a different perspective, remember what you did last time this happened that worked, think of someone who can help, or realize that this is part of an old pattern you don't need to keep repeating. Incremental improvements are the aim of this work.

You can call upon a whole range of helpers when you're in trouble. It's okay to use forceful words when you need to. Try this: "I call upon the assistance of all my guides and all the angelic hosts, ancestor spirits, ascended masters, and star beings of highest light to help me with (whatever) right now. I ask that the assistance continue unceasingly until the issue is resolved.

I ask for support, comfort, and clear guidance for me and my family, in line with the free will of all, throughout the duration of this event. I need help right now, please. Thank you."

HOW TO ASK FOR HELP FOR OTHERS

WHEN SOMEONE YOU LOVE IS ill or in a dangerous situation, it's difficult to think clearly, let alone reach out for help or think about what to say when you ask.

Here's the thing: you can't tell the guides what to do for someone else—regardless of whether it's good or bad—without remembering that we all have free will and are sovereign souls having a human experience. That doesn't mean you can't ask for help on their behalf or send them love from the guides. There are several ways to do this, and I've included scripts to help you start.

Calling in the guides.

Call in all your guides of highest light, and the guides of the other person, in alignment with their free will, and ask for assistance to address the situation. Here's an example.

"I call upon all my guides of highest light, and all of (person's name)'s guides of highest light, in line with their free will. I ask for a miraculous healing of their physical issues, with ease and freedom from pain for their physical, mental, and emotional systems. I ask for their medical team to be guided as well, toward a healing resolution that brings blessings and grace for everyone involved, in alignment with the free will of all."

Sending light to someone.

You can send light to another person; you just send it to their higher self instead of their physical self. Why? We all have soul lessons that we came in to complete. If someone is experiencing trauma, they might be in the middle of resolving a long-standing issue. We need to give them compassion and the freedom to do this. I know how hard this can be! I've been there several times with family or friends who are critically ill. Here's how you might say this:

"I call upon my guides of highest light and the guides of (name of the other person). I send love to their higher self for the resolution of this situation. I ask that they be wrapped in the highest light and love, surrounded, supported, guided, and protected unceasingly until this situation is resolved in line with their highest good. I ask for support for their family and friends, and I ask that I too be supported as part of this to accept the outcome with compassion and grace. I call upon their guides and mine to give them support, comfort, and freedom from pain and fear throughout this process. I ask the archangels and all their guides to be with them, holding them, and I call in the highest healing and love and blessings. So be it."

Asking for support for a child.

If you're the parent of a young child or one who is not of legal age, you can request this assistance for them as their parent. You just add that into your initial request: "As the parent of this child, I call forth (whatever guides you're calling)." Then continue with the request as usual. You can also ask for healing of your entire family as part of this process so everyone gets some support, comfort, and love. If you want to ask for assistance for a child who isn't yours, or for an adult child, you can use the same phrasing as noted above for another person, adding in the detail about free will. "I call upon all my guides of highest light, and all of (person's name)'s guides of highest light, in line with their free will. I ask for a miraculous healing of their physical issues, with ease and freedom from pain for their physical, mental, and emotional systems. I ask for their medical team to be guided as well, toward a healing resolution that brings blessings and grace for everyone involved, in alignment with the free will of all."

Supporting someone going through a tough challenge.

This can be someone who's dealing with a difficult situation such as mental illness, addiction, or ongoing pain and whose condition is making it hard for you to deal with them, but you don't want to cut them out of your life. Please note the other scripts for healing and support that could bring them some help; here's a script to bring some relief and help to both of you.

"I call upon all my guides of highest love and the guides of (person's name). I ask for healing light to surround and support them as they are during (whatever it is, or you can just say 'these difficult times'). I ask for patience and compassion as they deal with this, and I ask that they be guided to address the issues as best they can at this time. May they be blessed with love and support. Please let me know how to continue to hold them and their soul in light, even when it's hard for me to feel this on the physical plane. I ask for solid energetic boundaries around me as I learn how to keep them in my life and maintain my sovereign energetic space at the same time. I also ask for guidance to understand their role and the lessons they bring me in this life, and for support and assistance to release any energies or beliefs I have that contribute, however unknowingly, to their issues or the difficulties between us. I ask for wisdom and grace that we may both experience as much relief and release as possible at this time. Thank you."

Addressing relationships with love.

There's an energy practice of sending light to someone's soul when you're having difficulties with them on the physical plane. I use this one a lot, and it's helped multiple times to transform the relationships I have with people. Here's an example: I had a rough childhood, in part due to my mother's parenting style. This probably applies to most of us with one at least one parent, or whoever was or wasn't functioning in a parental role. I wanted to create a more comfortable, less stressful relationship with my mother, but I knew that trying to talk with her directly wouldn't work. So I started sending love to her higher self—nothing on the physical plane, just to her higher self. After a few months of doing this, our relationship changed. She is now more loving and respects my boundaries (usually), and I do the same for her. I've continued to work on this with her for years, whenever I feel it's necessary or helpful, while working on my own issues related to family at the same time. It's always good to look at how I may be contributing, however unknowingly, to a situation.

This is not a one-and-done approach. Think of it as more of a course correction than an immediate solution, and that might help you set your expectations.

When I want to support someone over a long period of time, by keeping them safe, for instance, I will send them love whenever it occurs to me over a period of months. I do this with my sons all the time: I send love to their souls and set the intention for them always to be safe in their homes, while driving, and at work. I set the intention for them to be healthy, happy, and doing what they love while making great money at it. I call in my guides and their guides, and then give thanks.

WHAT TO DO IF NOTHING SEEMS TO BE HAPPENING

I'VE BEEN ASKED WHAT TO do if nothing seems to be shifting and you aren't seeing any results. Here are some things to check.

- Are you open to being guided? Are you asking with a clear and quiet mind and paying attention so you can pick up on possible answers?
- Are you asking for help in a way that details what you need without telling your guides how it should happen? You need to know what you want help with, but it's not your job to tell them exactly how you want it resolved. Remember that resolution, answers, or relief can come without you knowing how or exactly what happened.
- Are you open to receiving help or an answer in unexpected ways?
- Are you asking for another person in alignment with their free will? It could be that their soul has chosen for them to experience this lesson. You can ask for them to

be supported, but you can't decide what needs to happen for them.

- Sometimes we have to understand and address a lesson before a situation can be resolved. Do you understand the lesson that's part of what you want help with?
- Sometimes we need to surrender to the timing of a resolution. Let the request go and wait for guidance or an indication of your next step. Believe me, I know how hard this is. I end up asking for help to accept and surrender to the divine timing of the resolution.
- If nothing else works, ask again for guidance to be clear and easily understood, and ask for a sign your guides are with you. Then be open to what happens.

FORGIVENESS

LEARNING TO FORGIVE PEOPLE FOR ways they've harmed me, and letting it go, has been one of the biggest blessings of my life. It's not about accepting what they did, whitewashing it, or pretending it didn't impact me. It's about choosing how to relate to whatever happened so it no longer defines or constrains me.

I'm a survivor of childhood rape, emotional and physical violence, and a narcissistic marriage partner. I made bad decisions for decades until I learned to release old beliefs and patterns about my self-worth and forgive those who inflicted suffering upon me.

I'm not glossing over this process; it can take a while, and it can be painful. I am saying that it can be supported and made easier with help from your guides. Their support isn't meant to replace the significant role that therapy can play in this journey, but you can ask your guides to assist you in finding the perfect professional to help.

In my experience, forgiveness creates a huge release of energy and it frees up space in your heart and mind to focus on what's most important to you, so I recommend considering the practice below.

If you're not ready to forgive the person(s) who caused you harm, you can forgive yourself for any way in which you blame yourself for what happened, whether consciously or unconsciously. The section on self-forgiveness is next.

TRY THIS

If this practice sounds like something you'd benefit from, know that it can be used for specific incidents or for a whole relationship. We all have energetic connections with other people, some of them subconscious, and it's good to break and release those that are no longer for our highest good. That's why I'm including text that calls for the breaking of any energetic patterns between you in this sample script.

"I call upon all my guides of highest light, my healing guides, and my guides of compassion and forgiveness for support. I call upon the soul of (name of person). I set the intention that any energetic connections, known or unknown, with (this person) which are not for my highest good be completed now, never to return to me in this lifetime. I set the intention for all my energetic bodies to be healed and sealed from the impacts of these interactions, with ease and grace for all aspects of my being. I set the intention to release any fears, anger, despair, or depression related to their actions, and ask for the healing love of forgiveness to bless me and free me from my outdated connections to them. I ask for the comfort, safety, and security of my guides to surround and support me."

Forgiving yourself.

This one might be hard for you. It's been a tough one for me. But it gets easier as you work with your guides to develop more compassion for yourself and your mistakes. Their nonjudgmental love helps a lot. Here's a script.

"I call upon my guides of compassion and forgiveness. Please help me stop shaming and blaming myself for the mistakes I made. Help me be kind to myself; help me honor the lessons I've learned from my mistakes and the changes I've made as a result. Help me remember that we all make mistakes, I just don't see others' errors in the same critical light I shine on myself. Surround me with comfort and love so I know everything is all right. Help me release these judgments and be at peace with all my past, including my mistakes. Many thanks for your love and guidance."

Asking for forgiveness.

This is a practice used to address energies between you and another person you want forgiveness from. Note: This isn't only for trauma or emergencies; it can be used to heal all of your relationships. It comes from a traditional Hawaiian practice of using forgiveness to bring things back into balance called *ho'oponopono*. This translates as "I'm sorry, please forgive me, I love you, thank you." I use the concepts but not the Hawaiian word since I don't speak the language and I'm not from that culture. Our words have power when we understand them, so it's best to say them in the languages we speak. This approach respects Hawaiian culture as well.

Basically, you connect to someone's energy and ask for forgiveness and resolution of any energies between you related to a certain situation. Here's an example.

"I call upon the higher self of (name of person). For any way that I am connected to you related to (whatever the issue is), I'm sorry, please forgive me, I love you, thank you." You repeat this, with meaning, until you feel some completion. You can do it once or repeat the process multiple times, whatever feels right.

I was a single mom and made decisions that I felt were the best at the time but in retrospect were not. My inner critics gleefully jump on these mistakes in the middle of the night or when I'm feeling down about something else. I use this process to address the situation by sending love and light to my kids instead of feeling terrible about myself, and I use it every day.

Here's a script I've used as a parent. Revise it to fit your needs.

"I call upon all my guides of highest light and the higher self of (person). For all the times when I was unavailable because I was working too much or exhausted, for all the times when I was unable to hold you or play with you or give you the attention you needed, I'm sorry, please forgive me, I love you, thank you. For all the times when I didn't realize you weren't getting the support you needed or was depressed and unable to give you the love that I felt, I'm sorry, please forgive me, I love you, thank you."

TRY THIS

I'm sure you can think of someone you could say this script to. It's an amazing form of healing, release, and empowerment. If nothing else, it frees up your energy so you can direct it positively instead of dwelling on things you wish were different. You can use this generic script for just about anything:

"I call in all my guides of highest light, and I reach out to the higher self of (person's name). For any ways that I am contributing to (issue), I'm sorry, please forgive me, I love you, thank you." Repeat as many times as needed, as often as needed.

I'm spending so much time on forgiveness because it's a powerful release. I do this forgiveness script whenever something I regret or that I'd like to be able to change comes up. Instead of feeling shame about it, judging who I was in the situation, or letting my inner critics dig into me, I send energy to resolve it. That action feels like it transcends time.

The next chapter builds upon our work to help those who are ill or suffering and addresses things we will all experience: death and dying. There's a great deal of help at hand to support us and our loved ones during those transition times.

CHAPTER 9
SUSTAINED SUPPORT DURING ILLNESS, DYING, AND DEATH

JULY 2021. MY BROTHER HAD a motorcycle accident overnight and is in intensive care. I'm heading to the hospital and have just crossed the border from Minnesota into Iowa when I feel his presence with me, floating above the car. I start talking to him, telling him that I'll help him whether he decides to go or to stay.

I call in every guide I can think of while I'm driving and request support, that he be free of pain, and that the healing or transition be easy for him. I don't have the same view of death as most people; I've helped people pass and know that we move into the light (at our own pace) and that only joy and love await us. Death brings freedom from pain and release from judgments, failures, and fears. I prefer that he die rather than be unconscious or nonfunctional long-term, and at this point, I don't know what his chances of recovery might be.

He never regains consciousness, and we removed life support a few days after the accident. Even knowing what I do about our expanded selves, it's devastating and so painful to let him go. I haven't been the kind of sister I wanted to be—I've been too caught up in my own life to celebrate his—and we'd grown apart these last few years before the accident.

My brother is an organ donor, so we're in the operating room waiting for him to die, and they will quickly harvest his organs. It's me, my mom, my sister, and two of his best friends. Several nurses are there as well, watching his vital signs.

We sing songs he loves. He's peaceful and does not struggle to breathe, which is great because they said he might after the breathing tube was removed and that would be excruciating to watch. My mom was a nurse, and it would be horrible for her to experience that and be unable to do anything for her youngest child and only son.

I sense his guides, angels, and archangels filling the room, waiting, and watching. After about twenty minutes I close my eyes and see his soul beam out of him like the sun, all over the room. Archangel Gabriel gathers him up and the archangels carry him home. His breathing stops and he passes gently, from one breath to the next. Even after we leave the operating room, I feel the archangels carrying him into higher and higher levels of light, bypassing places where he might have stayed, thinking he didn't deserve to move on. He is held, cocooned, carried as one most dear. Knowing this helps me get through the funeral and support my mom in her grief.

Here's a final note on my brother. A few months after he passed, he came to me in a meditation, healed, happy, and glowing. I cried, apologizing again for my regrets, and he stopped me and said, "I only remember the love. That's what I remember, all the love."

Worries and concerns about pain, long-term illnesses, and dying, and fears about what happens afterward, affect all of us in one way or another. I started this chapter with a story that in some ways has a positive ending, but the pain of that loss touches me every day even though I know my brother is at peace.

Whether you came to this chapter directly from the table of contents or are working steadily through the book, the practices outlined so far related to learning to ask for and recognize guidance can provide a scaffolding of support during times when it's difficult to think clearly. The practices shared in this chapter are like what I included in the last chapter on trauma and troubles, but more focused on support needed for a long-term issue.

The scripts I share here can also be helpful with many kinds of illnesses, not just physical ones. Severe depression, chronic illness like long COVID-19, dealing with family patterns of poverty consciousness, the psychological impacts of war, sexual violence, and racist or homophobic attacks: all of these too can have sustained impacts on your mental, emotional, and physical bodies, and the practices shared here focus on getting you support as you deal with them in the long-term.

These practices can also be used for issues related to finances, career concerns, or relationship woes—anything you've been dealing with for a while. When I was going through my divorce it felt like part of me was dying, even though divorce was my idea. Outdated beliefs and assumptions about how my life would go, who I was as a woman, what it meant to be loved, and whether I could be loved were all dying, and I leaned into what I share here to support me in that death, too.

This chapter will be heavy on scripts and light on discussion. The fears surrounding these topics can feel so heavy. While they are universal, the ways they appear in our lives are so specific to each of us that I don't want to comment, I just want to share ways to feel support.

The ability of the guides to cocoon us, hold us, bathe us in comfort and love comes to the forefront in their sustaining support, and can be requested to continue unceasingly when that is really needed. Use the basic steps outlined in Chapter 6 to get grounded, create a safe space, and set your intention to get the support you request in ways that are clear and easily understood. Then dive into the scripts.

ASKING FOR HELP WITH ONGOING ISSUES

I ALWAYS START REQUESTS FOR help with the archangels, since it is part of their primary purpose, and they're always around all of us. I call in Archangels Michael, Raphael, and Gabriel for healing and calming. I ask for Kuan Yin and the Goddess Isis to be present if I need serenity and the comfort of knowing I'll have strength to lean into while a situation gets resolved. This helps me, too, when something is out of my hands. Sometimes we must go through a tough time to break a pattern or as part of a lesson, and we may need to allow loved ones to do the same.

When we ask for powerful help, it comes in powerful ways: the arrival of unexpected relief and comfort, miracles popping up, the guides making their presence clearly known. Be open to getting answers to your prayers through the actions of others on the physical plane. Perhaps someone you love is ill and a great doctor or new treatment comes, or they have an unexpected, rapid recovery. Or you get support from a friend or counselor to let a loved one go if they are suffering. Maybe protection arrives when you are feeling unsafe, or money shows up out of the blue to get you through a crisis.

Let's go into some specific scripts for instances like this.

LONG-TERM ILLNESS

I SUFFERED FROM DEPRESSION AND deep despair for many years, sometimes getting to the point where I felt suicidal. My guides always gave me immediate support and bathed me in love when I reached out during those times.

I've watched friends suffer from long-term, debilitating illnesses and helped bring them healing energies. Exhaustion, fear, and pain can make dealing with a long-term illness even more difficult. In these instances, you can ask that any support provided by your guides be unceasing and strong enough for relief.

Be open to guidance coming in unexpected ways or through other people, such as new doctors, treatments, or medications. It's important to ask for peace, ease, and freedom from pain, discomfort, and fear. Pay attention to your body, as wisdom and guidance can come through your body or be most easily perceived through your body.

Sometimes you need to be asleep for miracle healings to occur. You can ask for a full range of healing modalities to be applied to your illness, including any healing technologies from star beings. In my experience, it's best to ask for these healings to take place while you are sleeping so your mental processes don't get in the way of their work.

Here's a sample script to begin with. Use what's helpful and ignore what isn't.

"I call upon all my guides of highest light and healing power. I ask for support to find treatments that bring me healing and relief from discomfort, pain, and fear. I set the intention to receive healing using the most advanced techniques available from the full range of healing guides available. I am open and ready to receive miraculous healing. I am open and ready to feel peace and ease as part of my support from all my guides. I ask to understand the lessons behind my illness, and for assistance in addressing any energy patterns related to those lessons so the issues can be resolved, released, and healed. Please help me feel your comfort and love, and the energy and strength to handle the symptoms and issues related to my illness. I am deeply grateful for this support. Thank you."

Ask to be held. Keep asking. Pay attention to any inner critics telling you that healing isn't possible, that you don't deserve to feel better, or that you need to just shut up and bear it. These are limiting beliefs that you can release, and you can ask for help with that.

"I ask to be unceasingly cocooned in light, held in love, guided, and comforted as I heal. I ask for help in understanding how to deal with and heal from this illness and best support my body in the healing process. I ask for help releasing any outdated beliefs and thought patterns related to my ability to heal and be free of pain, discomfort, and fear, and to replace those beliefs with the knowledge that I can receive miraculous healing and that my body is capable of great transformation. I am open to receiving healing on all levels, planes, and dimensions of my consciousness with ease, grace, flow, and joy in my mental, emotional, and physical bodies. Thank you."

TERMINAL ILLNESS

IF YOU OR A LOVED one have received a diagnosis of a terminal condition, you can still use the scripts above and ask for a miracle healing. You can also shift your focus to being free of pain and fear, held, comforted, and guided through the upcoming transition.

When my brother had his accident and I read up on brain injuries, I realized that he would never be the same and asked, in line with his free will, for him to be free of suffering and supported in whatever process his soul chose, including leaving his body. I asked that he be free of pain. This was an ongoing prayer.

It's okay to repeatedly request assistance when you need it. We are the ones in bodies, dealing with all this 3D stuff that the guides don't experience, so when it's important, I call upon the assistance of all the hosts of heaven to attend to someone I love and keep them free from discomfort, pain, and fear. Here's a script to use and revise as best fits your situation.

"I call upon all the hosts of heaven, all healing guides, all modalities, and all treatments to ease, grace, and bless (person's name, or 'me' if this is for you). I request this assistance for freedom from pain and fear, and that your support, comfort, guidance, and love bathe and cocoon them unceasingly, while awake and asleep. May they receive comfort on the physical plane from their medical team. May they be blessed with the remembrance of the beauty and love they have received and given and know that they are deeply loved and held by angels during this time. I ask for the love surrounding them to be so strong that they feel its power to free them of discomfort and fear moving forward. Bless them with ease and comfort. Thank you."

DYING AND DEATH

I HAVE A STORY TO share that might bring comfort if you or someone dear to you is dying or has passed. I had a private client ask me to have a session with her mother, who was afraid of dying. The client asked me to bring in her mother's guides, talk to them, and share any messages they had. I said yes but wasn't sure she would be open to what came through as she was a devoted Catholic and attended mass every day. Her daughter assured me it would be okay.

When I went into my meditation to call in her guides, I was amazed. I saw a long stream of angels, hundreds of angels, lined up and passing in front of her, placing a hand on her heart and blessing her for her devotion and faith. This went on and on and on. I shared how deeply loved she was, how honored she was for her faith and her commitment, and how blessed she was by the love in her heart. I don't remember all the details, but the vision was astoundingly beautiful. I heard later that she loved it and listened to the recording many times. Her whole family listened and was moved by it. She felt comforted by the session and passed in peace.

We can all pass in peace. Here's a sample script for the process of dying.

"I call forth my guides of the highest light as we move into the transition process, so (person's name) is carried home to the light encased and enrobed in divine grace. I ask this for all levels and planes of their consciousness, mind, body, and soul, in support of their soul's passage back to the light. May they know unceasing peace and ease through this process. May they receive support on the physical plane from their medical team, caregivers, and family to bring them comfort and freedom from pain. I call upon Archangels Michael, Gabriel, and Raphael and their angelic hosts to free them from fear, lift them up, and carry them home, back to the highest light in line with their divine soul mission. May they be blessed by this; may they know their soul's worth and how deeply loved they are. May they transition in full knowledge of their divine beauty and light. Thank you."

Love we send someone is never wasted, so you can continue to pray for someone's soul to be supported in moving into their highest expression of light even after they have died.

You can't change what happened to a loved one who passed traumatically, but you can send light to their soul and ask the guides—the Archangels Michael, Gabriel and Raphael and their angelic hosts in particular—to comfort their soul and heal them of residual fears.

GRIEF

YOUR GUIDES CAN SUPPORT YOU in your grieving process, through all of its stages. A popular model of grief considers five stages: denial, anger, bargaining, depression, and acceptance. Another model notes seven stages: shock and denial, pain and guilt, anger and bargaining, depression, the upward turn, reconstruction and working through, and acceptance and hope. No matter which model you think best applies to your situation, asking for support can help you through the entire process.

Grief is held in your body, so incorporating movement and soothing rituals can help you process it and put you in a better position to perceive the help you have right at hand. Here's a general script to help you process and release your grief:

"I'm asking for the help of my guides of highest love. I am in so much pain in my grief. I feel so much anger, guilt, and regret. Please help me understand how to process and release these feelings and how to find the energy to keep going and take care of the things I need to attend to. Please help me sleep, and please help me quiet my mind so I can stop focusing on this. Fill my heart with ease. I ask for guidance that is easily perceived and understood, and to be unceasingly held in love as I begin to heal. Please bring me inspiration and support on the physical plane as part of this process, too. Thank you. I am grateful for the help."

SETTING AN INTENTION FOR YOUR OWN DEATH

ARE YOU AFRAID OF DYING? Many people are. But it can be a time of great blessing and freedom from pain, constraints, worries, and fears. You can set an intention to be supported and carried home to the light and repeat this whenever you feel worried or afraid. Here's a script.

"I call upon all my guides to help me release my fears of dying. I set the intention to be free of fear and pain as I transition out of this body. I ask that any old patterns of judgment and fear of rejection I have related to dying be released now and replaced with the clear knowledge and trust that I am deeply loved, worthy of love, and moving back to the love that I came from. I ask that I be carried home to the light in beauty, joy, and remembrance of the glory of my soul. May I be blessed in my transition as I return to those I love who have gone before me. Please hold me close, carry me, comfort me, and bring me to grace. Thank you."

SETTING THE INTENTION FOR
A POSITIVE AGING PROCESS

I'D LIKE TO END THIS chapter on a proactive note. There's no reason we can't plan to age gracefully and joyfully. I'm finding the aging process to be incredibly freeing. The older I get, the less attached I am to anyone's opinions of me, the more compassion I have around the mistakes I've made, and the more I learn to love myself. It's easier and easier to focus on what I want to create with joy, what I love doing, and what allows me to move through my days (at times) in a state of bliss. It's easier and easier for me to sit in my garden, anchor light, call in my guides, and beam out bliss to help raise the baseline frequency of the planet. Many days, it's enough to feel the light of my expanded self, flowing through me.

I know that my mental and physical health could be challenged as I age, but this is not a certainty and I have medical professionals and healers to help if this happens. I intend to remain healthy and happy until I transition in peace, free of pain. I have no fear of death, so I don't add freedom from that to my intentions, but you can add it to yours.

Are you planning for a joyful last phase of your life? What does your body want to share with you about the process? If you fear you might be stiff and have limited mobility, work on increasing your flexibility and incorporate stretches and other practices now that will support your body more. Are you worried about your mental processes? What a gift the internet is for us, so we can research the latest developments and tried-and-tested tips related to cognitive resilience.

What else are you worried about? Finances? Ask the guides to bring you financial experts to support you, and tell them to bring more abundance your way, too. Check your assumptions and old family patterns here: Are you assuming, because of what your family says and believes, that your life must end in poverty and fear? You know better than that now; you can ask for help and be proactive about releasing those beliefs and setting an intention to have a healthy, happy, joyful, creative, free, inspiring, sovereign, expansive life in the time remaining to you.

Choosing to be positive and proactive about what we want and creating a life that supports this is a rebellious act, and it's a revolutionary act in the face of all the fear and negative messages about aging. It anchors energy for living life differently and helps others access the power to create the lives they want.

I intend to fulfill my potential for joyful creativity and share as much love as I can with people and the planet for the rest of my life. I intend to embody the energies and power of the Divine Feminine to my fullest capacity, to create a more just and peaceful world. That's how I'm planning the remaining time I have on Earth. How about you?

FROM THE GUIDES

One of our strongest hopes is that we may support you in knowing that your transition can be an opening to a peace you might have never experienced on Earth.

So many of us come to hold you specifically during your time of transition. As you read this, we are closer than we've been since you began this book. You are so loved.

You are held. You are treasured. We surround you to guide you, to carry you, to whisper that all is well. We will be with you during the entire transition process. Ask us to help you release fears. Ask for our help to bring you relief from pain. Ask for our help to feel all the love in your life from family, friends, the beauty of the earth, and all of us, so close around you. We touch your hair, we kiss your cheek while you are sleeping, and we await with joy your transition back into your body of light so that we may greet you as a friend, loved one, and family most divine.

You are so deeply loved, so held, so treasured, so honored for the resilience and power in your heart. May you be blessed by your reading of these words and feel us wrap you in love right now.

What comfort in that message! This was a heavy chapter. Let's have a palate cleanser in the next one, which is all about how to find more ease, flow, and joy in your life through working with your guides.

CHAPTER 10
MORE EASE, FLOW, AND JOY

MAY 2011, MY FIFTIETH BIRTHDAY. I make a commitment to myself to focus more on my creativity and letting things be easy. I've just completed a short story writing course that sparked my creativity in joyful, playful, magical ways. I feel more confident and comfortable with myself. Life has some breathing room and flow. My work with my guides is strong, fun, supportive, and adventurous. They feel like family. They are my family.

From the first time I sensed them while sitting in the bathtub all those years ago, I felt joy and comfort flowing from them. These feelings became stronger once I got divorced and their comfort and support helped me get through the day. As I reclaimed who I was, joy was an undercurrent carrying me forward. My guides strengthened my resilience and helped me to see beauty and release tension. They expanded my idea of what is possible, reminded me of my gifts and strengths, and helped me sense my soul light.

Eventually, I was able to tap into my expanded self and then sustain that for longer periods of time. My expanded self—my intuition and higher self—brings freedom, creativity, power, confidence, exuberance, serenity, strength, resilience, perseverance, and joy to every aspect of my life.

I've stopped pushing against life. Instead of fighting with it, mentally deciding what is needed no matter how difficult, I approach an issue or situation by looking at what I want and asking, "How I can make this easy? How can I quickly resolve this situation?" I pay attention to which doors open and which doors stay stuck when I push so I can pivot and look at other options. I keep asking for help to get what I want with ease, grace, flow, and joy.

The techniques I shared in Chapters 1 through 8 help you make room for more joy and set you up to experience more of your expanded self. The incremental improvements you make by using these techniques not only raise your resonant frequency, so you experience joy more often; they also bring you the confidence and clarity to detach more quickly from whatever holds you back, so you automatically embody more of your soul light.

What does that feel like? It's a lot more fun than struggling!

I share details and scripts below so you can begin to incorporate more ease, flow, and joy into your life. When you hang out with your guides, your vibration naturally rises to be in closer resonance with theirs; you harmonize with them (you're in resonant harmony with them). Not completely, but there's a definite increase in the light and love you carry inside you.

This makes everything easier. Lower, negative energies and patterns can't cling to you, and you recognize them more quickly. You're better equipped energetically to call in support and to recognize it—it's like tuning a radio from static to a station with a strong reception.

You can ask for help to raise your frequency as you ask for the other support you need. And when you're feeling good, ask for help to sustain it. The main difference between what I share in this chapter and what we've looked at earlier in the book is that these practices help sustain what feels great, what we appreciate, and what keeps us going.

I've pulled together topics and approaches below that we haven't covered yet so you can see additional ways to apply what we've already covered, and work with the guides who are already around you to help make your life a little better every day.

Let's dig in so you can see what I mean and start using what seems fun.

DAILY PRACTICES FOR STAYING BALANCED AND SERENE

IN THIS SECTION, I SHARE specific things I do every day to stay balanced and serene (for the most part). It's not necessary to do all of them—see what works best for you.

Mantras.

A mantra is a word or phrase used to put your mind in a calm, meditative state. A simple mantra can help you maintain your positive outlook and address your desires with confidence. I use mantras to focus my thoughts and energy on what's important to me, and to set up the vibration of what I want but might not have yet.

Two short mantras I use throughout the day are "Everything's all right" and "I'm fully supported in all ways and always."

I created a long, rhythmic mantra to use while I'm walking the dog. You could use parts of this or take it as inspiration to create your own walking mantra. Here it is.

"I'm so richly blessed and abundantly free,
I always have so much more than I need.

In opulent flow, I create joyfully.
I always have all the inspiration I need.

With my family and guides so supportive of me,
I always have all the love I need.

I'm vibrantly healthy, limber, and lean.
I always have all the youthful energy I need.

In restful repose, I relax gracefully.
I always have all the time I need.

I'm so blessedly rich, sovereign, and serene.
I always have all of everything I need."

TRY THIS

What mantra might work for you? It could be one word or phrase, or you could use an image associated with a word to bring yourself peace. You could create a longer mantra like I did (or use whatever parts of mine you like). You can find traditional mantras connected with religious or yogic practices online, or you look for other affirmations or phrases that calm you.

Manifesting.

Many people focus on manifesting what they want by deliberately choosing thoughts, feelings, and energy that are in alignment with what they want—the energy of already having it. You may have heard this referred to as "deliberate creation" or "following the law of attraction." It ties into what we talked about earlier in the book: holding a vision of what you want, feeling and imagining that it's already true, and adding sensory details to the vision so you resonate more closely with what you want. You aren't searching for it, grasping at it, or hoping it will come true; you are embodying how it feels when you have it, luxuriating in it.

I work with manifesting a lot, staying focused on what it will feel like once I get what I'm looking for and adding as many sensory details to my imaginings as possible without attaching too much energy or effort to the exact outcome in case what shows up isn't how I imagined it (it's frequently better). I've done this to lose weight, to get free of debt, and even to find the perfect pair of boots. Boots are serious business in Minnesota in the winter, so finding exactly what I wanted and available in my size made me very happy.

You can imagine what you want to manifest (a new job, money for a home, a healthy family, someone who loves you just as you are) and call in the support of your guides at the same time to not only help make this dream come true, but also help you raise your vibration so you can align more quickly with the desired end result. This works for everything:

- Flow
- Creativity
- Financial abundance
- New opportunities
- Loving relationships
- A happy family
- Vibrant health
- Travel and adventure

TRY THIS

Here's a script for manifesting.

"I call upon all my guides of highest light to support me in creating and maintaining a vibration of having (what you want). Help me hold the energy, images, feeling, and sense of already succeeding in having this. Help me hold the perfect degree of focus, keeping the energy flowing toward the creation of what I want and sustaining it without striving or worrying about it. Please help me understand and act in ways that support the joyful creation and experience of what we're manifesting together. Thank you."

Here's another one to try:

"I call upon all the beings of highest light who work with me. I set the intention to be energetically supported as I imagine having/being (whatever you're looking to manifest). Please help me to manifest this as I imagine it or even better, and to do it with ease, grace, flow, and joy. Please bring me inspiration and ideas for how to manifest my wishes quickly and joyfully. I'm grateful for the support and ask that it continue unceasingly until I receive what I'm drawing to me."

FEELING GRATITUDE AND PEACE

THE FOLLOWING PRACTICES AREN'T THINGS I do with my guides or ask them about, they're part of what I bring to the table when I collaborate with my guides and part of what I do to raise my vibration to carry more light so I'm a good partner in the work we do together. Plus, these practices just help me get through each day feeling as positive as possible.

Feeling grateful.

This is a huge one for me. I've lived in places where life is extremely difficult for people, especially women and children, where they don't have clean air or water or access to food, education, or safety.

How easy I have it—clean water and air, access to food, freedom of speech. Everyone I love is safe and healthy. I can explore and create as I please. I have many opportunities to freely share my writing and spiritual thoughts.

And so many choices. One of the things that astounded me when I came home from the Peace Corps was the grocery store aisles. I'd find myself just standing and staring in amazement at all of the different breakfast cereals or brands of dog food.

I don't have a specific gratitude practice as much as a running thread of giving thanks throughout the day. My mom laughs at how frequently I say how grateful I am for coffee and that we don't have to grow it, roast it, grind it, or sell it. How amazing it is, how grateful I am that I can get coffee I love all over the place.

What do you have in your life that's like that? When my kids were little, I was thankful every day for a working washer, dryer, and dishwasher in the house. Access to the internet, good doctors, and easily available meds. Notice what makes life easier for you and what brings you joy or safety.

Gratitude is another high-frequency emotion, so the more you feel it, the closer you get to your guides' resonance of love and light and the more they can help you.

Creating.

I get grumpy and frustrated if I'm not using my energy in creative ways almost every day. That can be through cooking, writing, dancing, playing music, or gardening.

Anything I do that creates beauty or joy counts for me (so dancing fits, even though I just do it for fun). Even planning for the creation counts, like reading a new cookbook or planning a new writing adventure. For me, creativity is one of the keys to staying centered in my heart and sustaining a positive flow of love in my life. How about you? What works for you?

Being in nature.

A great deal of my serenity comes from being in nature, sitting in my garden, watering plants, and feeding and watching the birds. Even watching nature documentaries and whale-watching videos or reading articles about nature sustains me. I studied forestry because trees are my favorite thing. Does nature calm and sustain you, too? If not, maybe there are other forms of beauty that do.

Appreciating beauty.

Another thing I make time for is mini beauty breaks. These can include wearing one of my vintage perfumes, watching a movie I love, reading the words of a great writer, getting lost in a story, or looking at home decorating or gardening magazines (don't judge). I make time for all of these things because they fuel me. When I downsized my home after the kids moved out, I curated my belongings so there is now something beautiful that I love everywhere I look, in every room. Does beauty fuel you, or is it something else? I include laughter and hugs in the beauty break category as they bring me joy (which to me is an expression of beauty).

Being the Queen Me.

This is my practice of feeling serenely sovereign. A few years ago, I realized that what I really wanted was to feel serene. Serenely wealthy, too, which for me is knowing that I always have all the resources I need to do everything I want (including time, money, creativity, power, health, energy, and focus). At the time, I didn't know what it would feel like for my normal reality to be fully resourced, so I binge-watched *The Crown* on Netflix. If anyone expects that it's normal to have a life of abundance, it's a queen.

So what happened? I tried on this vibe and discovered that I could lean into the support of my guides more easily. I found and moved into the most perfect place to live. I settled into a creative flow with my writing. I now feel richly blessed and blessedly rich. I am being the Queen Me—blissfully, creatively, serenely, and radiantly. Asking, "How can I feel serenely sovereign as I move through my day?" is now a part of my usual practice.

TRY THIS

What fuels and sustains you? What occurred to you as you read my notes above? What fuels your joy? Squeeze some of these into your day or add them to your practice if that helps.

HANGING OUT WITH MY GUIDES

WHILE MY INTERACTIONS WITH MY guides in my inner sanctuary can be adventurous, much of my time with them is just listening, relaxing, and seeing what comes up. It's not always about working on something or releasing old patterns and beliefs; just hanging out with them and resting in their energy renews me and fills me with peace. It's a blessing to be around them and all that love, and I wallow in it. ("Wallow" is one of my favorite verbs. Growing up in Iowa with all the pig farmers, it's understandable).

Continuing to expand and explore how much light and love I can carry in my body and looking at ways I can support people and the planet will be a daily focus with my guides for the rest of my life.

All of the practices outlined in this book help me focus my time and energy on what's most important to me while knowing I'm safe, supported, and free to expand and create in whatever ways feel joyful and powerful to me.

It's about choice: choosing to sense the light that's hidden from our visible world, choosing to feel supported even if I don't see a presence standing in front of me, choosing to trust in my intuition when it might not make logical sense, and choosing to believe that the world can be different, more just and equitable, and infused with pure love. I make these choices every day because I just can't accept that our external reality is all that's available and true.

Here's an affirmation I use at the beginning of the day to orient myself.

"I am an emanation of the divine light. I open now to receive that which by my divine destiny is given from the source of loving creation. I am an emissary of light. I open now to be all that I am, and to allow the manifestation of these divine gifts to fully flow through me for the wellness of the world, the wellness of my own body, and the loving presence of the divine light at work in my life. This is my affirmation of the light, and the invocation of my intention, manifest on all levels, planes, and dimensions of my consciousness. So be it."

TRY THIS

What process can you use to keep expanding your light and love in the world? How can you collaborate with your guides to take advantage of all the blessings and ease that are already in your life? You can use what I shared above, or here's another script to get you started.

"I call upon my guides of highest love to help me orient my day and energy to what feels truest to me and serves my highest good, no matter what's showing up on the news or in my life. I choose to trust in the love I sense from my guides and the truth of my intuition, and I ask for ongoing support in finding ways to share my soul gifts and strengths freely and joyfully. Thank you."

FROM THE GUIDES

Many of you are starting to open further to the light within and around you. The messages from and presence of your guides are available now to assist you in opening to greater joy and beauty in your life. It is not just about service and clearing out old energies— the exuberance you feel in the presence of the love we carry and share with you is part of your path as well. Bliss and joy are high frequencies, concentrated cleansers, and high-level nutrients for you and the planet.

If you love nature, beauty, art, or music, fill yourself with joy while you experience them and you will act like a beacon of light and nourishment for their further blooming. So much joy is inside and around you, filled with grace and peace and waiting to be shared with the world. Surrender to it when we are with you.

The next chapter builds upon these concepts and uses your imagination to create an inner sanctuary. It isn't necessary to use an inner sanctuary to work with your guides, but it's something I treasure about my own practice, so I included it.

CHAPTER 11
CREATE YOUR INNER SANCTUARY

Fall 1987. I'VE STARTED GETTING clear guidance and can sense some guides, but still struggle to quiet my mind so I can get a few minutes of peace. I even review the symptoms of schizophrenia and multiple personality disorders in medical texts because I feel so unbalanced by the voices of my inner critics.

I find a book by LaUna Huffines called *Bridge of Light*. In it, she discusses ways to use your imagination to create an inner sanctuary. I get one of her meditations on a cassette tape and listen to it like it's a lifeline, which it is. If I follow this meditation and visualize walking down a path, taking a boat, and then walking up a hill and entering a temple, my mind quiets for a bit. I run with it. It gives me hope that I might be okay. Her meditations don't solve my problems, but they give me some much-needed peace.

I keep playing with the visualization until I revise it to best fit me and find that the key is for the temple to have a huge wooden door that I can close, like in a medieval castle or a Moroccan souk—old wood, metal spikes and all. This, finally, shuts out the voices.

Once I'd created this, my work with my guides expanded, and most importantly, I started being able to release the emotions and mental programs that had kept me stuck and unhappy for so long.

The main way I used my inner sanctuary for at least a decade was to shut the door on the inner chatter and release the burdens of my worries about money and feelings of failure, exhaustion, and despair for a few minutes. Eventually, I did this by imagining a small one-room cabin with a rocking chair and a big fireplace, big enough for me to crawl into. I would ask my guides to help me, and sometimes the goddesses Isis or Kuan Yin were with me, though most of the time I didn't sense anything. When I felt really bad, I crawled into the flames and imagined them burning away all my troubles. I didn't feel the heat, but the image of release helped me.

An inner sanctuary is a safe space you imagine where you can go for a quiet break or for active work with your guides to receive inspiration, comfort, and answers. It's just using your imagination to envision a place where you can interact with your guides, especially if sitting in quiet meditation doesn't work for you. It never has worked for me, so I meet them in my inner sanctuary.

Creating this space is not necessary for working with your guides or understanding guidance, but my students enjoy learning about it. If it doesn't sound interesting to you, you can skip this chapter. If you enjoy playing with your imagination, you might love it.

This chapter explains how I created my inner sanctuary, imaginarium, or temple of light—however you want to refer to it—and how you can create something similar. I share a couple of different ways to do this, and of course you can revise them to fit your practice.

If you've found that a walking meditation or some other type of physical activity works best for you to commune with your guides, look at the second option under "Geometric Shape Sanctuary," as this can be a fun way to approach setting an energetic boundary. I use it when I want to make sure I'm not absorbing other people's energy.

THE POINT OF THIS IS PLAYFUL POWER

BASICALLY, THE INNER SANCTUARY IS a space or feeling you imagine in enough detail that you can return to it again later. The point is to create a space where you feel completely safe and able to turn off the world and turn up your imagination. When you allow your imagination free rein, you begin to feel the playful power of your expanded self, filling you up with luscious possibilities.

You can use your sanctuary to take a break from the stress of outer life and/or to let your mind, heart, and joyful creativity expand free of constraints. You can make it as simple as a quiet beach, a pair of rocking chairs on a porch, or however your imagination wants to run with.

HOW YOUR IMAGINATION AND AN INNER SANCTUARY CAN HELP YOU

IF YOU ENJOY USING YOUR imagination, your willingness to experiment with it can be the cornerstone of your spiritual practice. This can be so effective in your search for inner answers because as you gain peace and receive guidance in the sanctuary, you begin to experience the same things in your external life.

As you release limiting patterns, ancestral beliefs, and fears of your creative power in the sanctuary, you start to move through your days of laundry, cooking, and working with the same sense of release and inspiration.

What does your sanctuary bring to you? Here's what mine has brought me.

- My inner world is filled with magical adventures.
- I receive external validations that my internal shifts are working.
- I know without a doubt that I can get help from my soul and guides for everything.
- I feel empowered, blessed, and filled with gratitude every day.

How do you create your own inner sanctuary? I share two ways below; both are malleable, so you can mold them to work for you.

SETTING EXPECTATIONS

THIS MAY TAKE MORE TIME than anything else in the book, depending on how detailed you get and how easy it is for you to imagine. It takes more time because you are, in essence, building an energetic container to hold the frequency of your guides and your soul. It's a resonance chamber.

Because it takes repeated exposures to their frequencies to instill the energies of the guides in a space, it's not something you do once and check off a list. The buildup of resonance is the reason this practice can become so helpful, even if you just imagine sitting in the space. It's like a sauna of higher love without the heat.

You might jump right into this. Most of us work at visualizing a sanctuary space for a while to make it feel substantial and real and to anchor the details that support our experience. My students love entering my sanctuary in meditations, but not all of them end up using a sanctuary in the long run. That doesn't stop them from working with their guides.

I share this practice as it's been so effective and fun for me. You might want to read or listen to the whole chapter first and then come back to what seems intriguing and enjoyable for you to explore. Now that I've made you either warier or more curious, let's jump in.

CREATING YOUR INNER SANCTUARY

THIS BEGINS WITH IMAGINING A peaceful place that feels safe and calm. You make the place seem as real as possible. If you've visited a place like this on a vacation or from a favorite book in childhood (*The Secret Garden* is one example), you can just use that. The first step to creating your inner sanctuary is to find this place of peace, a landing area where your mind can rest and rejuvenate, a seat of solace. If spaces don't bring you peace, jump to the next section covering geometric shapes.

Find images that bring you the greatest peace and hold them so strongly in your mind that, with your eyes closed, you can see yourself experiencing this peace. Build in as many details as possible: what it looks like, smells like, and sounds like; the weather and the amount of sunlight; sounds from the wind, birds, or animals; how it feels to be there, what you're wearing, and where you're sitting or walking. Make it real. The more real it feels, the better it can serve you as a space for interacting with your guides.

Remember the vision of the future we started with? I'd like you to call up that vision, that feeling of being calm, confident, clear, able to create what you want, and fully receptive to guidance and the answers you seek, and we'll build upon that.

You might imagine sitting on a calm beach, surrounded by the sounds of the ocean. Or you might want the protection and privacy of a structure such as a house or a safari tent. You might imagine yourself in a stand of redwoods or floating on a boat in the middle of a calm lake.

My inner sanctuary has the cabin I mentioned, gardens I walk through, big trees I sit under, and forests I can see in the distance, as these images also bring me peace and I sometimes walk to these places and talk to my guides. What kinds of landscapes and structures bring you peace and make you feel expansive and joyful?

Once you've chosen your place of peace, I want you to imagine there's a short path leading away from it to a wall with a gate in it. See yourself walking up the short path to the gate. The wall is high enough that you can't see into the area. You open the heavy door, and the most beautiful, protected space is revealed, with a building that fits into the setting so perfectly it draws you in.

Look around: This is a place where you can feel safe, a space for inspiration, working with your guides, and dreaming of how you'll create a life and world you love. Stay here, rest here, and fill in as many details as seem fun right now. This isn't the only version of your sanctuary—you might find that the building gains rooms or the gardens and landscape expand—but feel a joyful peace here now. It's a great start.

Each time you want to return to this sanctuary, you can either start at the place where you began or close your eyes, touch your heart, and imagine you are immediately in the walled-in area. You will be—or you will be eventually, with practice. Don't put pressure on yourself to get that part instantly right. Your sanctuary is meant to be a playful, peaceful place, so sink into that and let it bless you.

If moving out of the initial peaceful place feels like a tug and you want to stay there, you can imagine some type of structure or space there. If you're on a beach, you can simply add a cave you can enter as your place of interaction. You might have structures there as well, like a tent, a cathedral, or a house with a courtyard and fountain. Use whatever imagery you find most inspiring and fun that pops easily into your imagination.

You can also ask your guides to help you imagine a space where it will be easiest for you to work together.

FROM THE GUIDES

Here's a message from Archangel Michael that expands upon how imagery can help you get started and gives some background on why this can be a powerful practice.

This is the story of starting an inner temple: Each soul meets with a family of guides before becoming embodied to set up key tasks, challenges, goals, and strengths for their life-to-be. The team of guides meets with the to-be-embodied soul several times before birth takes place. Along with goals and key challenges, resonance points are established: ideas and images that will serve to aid the soul in remembering its purpose and intentions. Images that bring the soul great peace are central to this idea of resonance points.

The wealth of available imagery on the internet is not only for the sharing of beauty and information about your world; it also serves as a menu of memory images—including computer-generated images of other, imagined worlds—for the wide range of embodied souls at this time. These images that touch hearts and minds can serve each soul as stepping stones in constructing and inhabiting their inner sanctuary.

Just as the physical body serves in part to contain the light of the soul, the inner sanctuary serves to contain the light of the family of guides accompanying the soul on this journey of embodiment.

These images help establish the frequency of connection between the body and the Family of Light accompanying each of you. This is by no means the only way to access your guides, but it is an implanted trigger that each of you can take advantage of. I am Archangel Michael, and I can be called upon to aid you in your imagination. Be at peace in this place now.

TRY THIS

Think about these questions and see what comes to mind.

- What images bring you great peace? The trigger for your sanctuary is not just beauty, but peace.
- What is your landscape, soundscape, or capsule of calm and serenity?

- How do you move through it? Are you resting in a shelter and looking out at it or walking in gracious gardens?
- How does water play a part in your sanctuary? How about fire, trees, scents, sounds, or the wind? Are there forests and animals in this space, or just a pristine structure?

YouTube videos, Instagram posts, and Pinterest images can be a source of inspiration here if you're a visual person or don't like to do quiet meditation. If you really enjoy playing with this, you can create many spaces in your sanctuary to support you. In my temple, there are many places to explore:

- A library with volumes of books and a massive table where the guides gather with me for teaching.
- A bathhouse and steam room for healing and releasing old patterns.
- A meadow with large oak trees where I lie in the grass and relax under a beautiful sky.
- A large home where I meet with a group of goddesses.
- Gardens to wander in (nature is obviously important to me).
- A large safari tent that looks out onto a savanna where I write and talk with my creative muses.

I work with a wide range of guides in my sanctuary in support of my dreams and creativity and as part of my work for the planet. I created a resource page on my website that includes a link to images for a sanctuary space or imaginarium. Check it out at https://julesapollo.com/extras if you'd like some inspiration.

IF THIS APPROACH DOESN'T WORK FOR YOU

I'M VERY VISUAL, SO MY inner sanctuary works like a movie that I'm watching and in at the same time. Maybe you're not as visual. Maybe the sense of touch is more important for you, and you imagine a sauna or a pool with water at the perfect temperature for relaxing. Maybe walking meditations work best for you, and you just check in, imagine your guides walking next to you, and allow inspiration to flow in.

I had a student who'd survived great trauma and didn't feel safe outside, even imagining being outside. We finally discovered that seeing herself within a golden sphere of protection from Archangel Michael while sitting on her bed, allowed her imagination to soar.

Something I've done during stressful times is close my bedroom door and call in the guides to surround me on my bed, telling them they have to come close as I'm too stressed out to do anything else. This might be perfect for you—if so, run with it.

If none of this works, there are videos on YouTube with sound and imaginary spaces—such as a cabin in a snowstorm or an old library with a roaring fire, the sounds of birds in a forest, or a rainstorm from inside a tent—that might be a place to start. You could go from there or just use the source video if that works.

Perhaps you're not visual but music or sounds really help you relax and enter expanded states. You can create a soundscape as an opening for guidance. It could include the sound of the ocean, songs of whales or birds, gentle rain, or a breeze through a forest. There are many soundtracks you can get—YouTube can be a great place to try different ones to see what you like—and you can purchase MP3s of hour-long rainstorms, for instance, quite inexpensively. I know many artists and authors who write while listening to specific soundtracks. I like to put on a soundtrack of whale songs when I'm moving through an airport to create a calming soundscape around me.

There's no need to go down a rabbit hole of research on this. It's best to start with whatever first entered your mind as you were reading this section that gets you to a place of peace so you can sense guidance.

If this approach seems silly or doesn't appeal to you, let's review the next one, as it's a completely different way of getting the same result.

GEOMETRIC SHAPE SANCTUARY

THIS IS AN APPROACH TO creating a safe space and sanctuary within an imagined, clear geometric shape or shelter you rest within. I use a sphere or a pyramid. This is an old spiritual practice, and many people use a cube called "the cube of space" to do this with different guides who are called in from each side of the cube. Read on to see what I mean: the guides describe it better than I can.

FROM THE GUIDES

The guides talk about geometric shapes and how using your intention and imagination while inside a shape creates a resonance chamber that further strengthens your actions. Essentially, it's using the power of the shape to support your work.

You may need to read through this or listen to it a few times, create your shape, and then come back to this as the approach is more advanced.

We begin with the recommendation that you pick a shape, a geometric form that you can rest inside, for energetic protection and inspiration. We recommend that you choose the first form that comes to mind. For some of you, it's a sphere. For others, it's a square. Some of you enjoy more complex forms.

See yourself inside a shape that encompasses your entire body. This is not made out of opaque material—what we would like you to see is clear sides or sides of clear crystal, if that is better for you.

Imagine you're in this clear glass or crystal shape and that all its sides are lit with a soothing white light. Some of you might hear a hum from this light, but it's not necessary to hear that.

As you move into this geometric form and use the frequency of the light you're imagining, you're setting up a resonance chamber. Each time you use your intention, it empowers the frequency within this form. And this is why we suggest working with it now. It is strengthened each time you use it as a safe space for when the world becomes a bit overwhelming.

Your imagination is a way to make your dreams manifest very quickly. You're taught to take your dreams and break them down into doable steps, but in your imagination, it's done, complete, you're already experiencing it. Your imagination can transcend time and space because you put your energy into the result of what you seek.

When you do this within a geometric form constructed with light and established by your frequency, the form concentrates the energetic support from your guides. When you call in your intention, you infuse this form with the energy of your soul as well as the energy of your guides. This is why we recommend this practice. It's an easy thing, it's powerful, and it can be playful. There is no way to do this wrong.

TRY THIS

First, choose a form to sit inside. I always use a sphere if I'm walking and a pyramid if I'm sitting, for no reason other than that's what I like. Let it settle, play with the size and the clarity of the materials for a bit. You can add light moving through the sides if this makes sense or leave it out. I usually don't see lights but rather intend for the form to be infused with the light and protective love of the archangels. I put a sphere around me if I'm going through a busy public space like a shopping mall or an airport and don't want to pick up energy from others. If you're an empath, someone who is sensitive to the energy of others, this is an easy way to preemptively protect yourself.

You can combine this imagery with the imagery of your sanctuary. I envision myself sitting in a crystal pyramid on a secluded beach with the soft sounds of waves in the background when I need to quickly calm my mind and body. This is one of the more playful ways to find some inner peace and get guidance, so have fun.

These peaceful places have sustained me in both joyful and difficult times and are part of the true power of this work for me. The next chapter talks about how you've changed since starting this book, what that means for making your big dreams and goals come true, and how you can help people and the planet in ways you may not have thought about before, the true power of this work for you.

CHAPTER 12
HOW YOU'VE CHANGED AND WHAT YOU CAN DO WITH IT

I'M NOT ONE OF THOSE spiritual people who never gets angry. These times fill me with rage at not being able to make a bigger impact or limit people's suffering, especially children's. Recently I was meditating on peace but got frustrated. It didn't feel like enough. I asked my guides for help, and here's what they said.

Become incandescent with your rage at the suffering of people and the planet. If that doesn't feel powerful enough, imagine your rage as light eruptions, geysers of light, tsunamis of light: the earth's power to reset and clear can be a guide and example at this time. Your light triangulates with the light of those you've called forth to reset energies, patterns, and light grids so they are infused with love and not the fears of small men driving patriarchal patterns. We are present here now. Call in, tap into, expand into the energies and help at hand to construct a new earth.

I love this message; I love hearing how we can use our rage proactively and work with our guides to change the world instead of feeling like we're stuck on the sidelines while it implodes. Here's a script I created from this message that I use when meditating on peace and the changes I feel are needed to create a just and sustainable earth.

"I am that I am. I call in all my guides of the highest light and love. I set the intention to anchor, into the air, the soil, and the waters, the power and love of a thousand suns to transmute the energies of war, genocide, injustice, hatred, and fear into a planetary grid of light so fiercely intense that it eclipses patriarchal patterns of control, illuminating Earth as a healthy and peaceful planet. So be it and so it is done."

I always ask for help from my guides to start shifting my energy when I'm frustrated. I limit my time on social media, so I can track what's going on in the world but leave once I start to get upset and before I dive into despair, which is a debilitating emotion for me. I note what's got me upset, and that's what I work on with the guides. Together, we anchor light to override lower energies and infuse the world with love and peace. This uses the support we all have at hand to help create a new reality.

CREATING A BETTER WORLD

NOW THAT YOU HAVE THE tools to work with your guides, I hope you'll use these tools to help make the world a better place. You're here now on this planet, in the middle of all this chaos, to use your energy and guides to help, so dig into this.

Here are the basic steps you can take.

- Note what's frustrating, angering, or hurting you about the state of the world now.
- Call in all your guides of the highest love.

- Set the intention for your combined energies and love to offset and override the conditions and actions you feel need to change to help people and the planet.
- Imagine all types of guides surrounding the planet, coming to help. See hosts of angels or lightships or massive groupings of spacecraft like those in Star Wars, whatever helps you feel there is power behind the energy you're calling in to help, light flowing into the planet to create lasting change.
- Keep coming back to this process whenever you find yourself frustrated, angry, or fearful.
- Trust that your intention and these energies are helping.

Are there actions you can take on the physical plane that pop into your head as you're doing this? Perhaps you can donate to causes, call your representatives, follow organizations that are helping, protest, or create art that expresses what you're feeling and envisioning.

Don't focus only on the negative actions causing you pain; make sure you use your love and the energy of your guides to imagine a better way. Again, use the phrase "what if." What if we lived on a peaceful planet where everyone's basic needs were met, where everyone had access to education and opportunities to share their gifts, wisdom, and creativity? What if the earth and the environment were respected and honored, and humanity learned from the wisdom and compassion of native cultures to live in harmony with nature?

Don't let your mind tell that you this is childish and not worth doing. Nothing has ever been created, invented, or built that wasn't first imagined and held as a viable vision.

My focus now and for the remainder of this life is to expand into embodying more of the exuberance of my soul. To be joyfully creative. To know that the power of the love I have in my heart for my friends and family, the compassion I have for those who suffer from inequality and a lack of adequate resources, and my commitment to the planet are all supported, empowered, anchored, and enlivened as I work with all my guides, my Family of Light, to fulfill my potential and be of service.

What you've read so far will help you get guidance in ways that best fit into your life and to trust the guidance you're getting. Once that happens, you'll start to feel some of what I described above because you'll embody more of your soul light, strengths, and power. Here's what I hope you come to know as truth and part of your everyday life:

- You're never alone; help is at hand whenever you need it.
- No matter what happens in your life, you have help to handle it.
- You're deeply loved, supported, guided, and held.
- You're worthy of being loved and of all good things coming to you.

YOU'VE CHANGED, NOW USE IT

YOU'RE NOT THE SAME PERSON who picked up this book, even if you didn't try everything and still wonder what you're sensing.

You have the tools to quiet your inner critics, forgive yourself, and rally support for every aspect of your dreams and goals. But it goes beyond that. You've had an operating system upgrade and it's time to put that to use. You're stronger, more resilient, and more aware of the ways you can apply the help at hand. You're in resonance with the guides around you.

The planet is messed up. Whole countries are in chaos and suffering is everywhere. Being an embodied soul at this time of great upheaval is a gift and a responsibility. There are many souls lined up, hoping for the chance to become embodied on the planet during these times of massive transformation, even for short periods of time.

You won the embodiment lottery. And now you can be an energy resistance worker by calling in peace, justice, and compassion with your morning coffee and seeing these energies fill up the planet like water in a well. Calling in the support of your guides, you can set the intention for your energy and time to be focused on activities and people in line with your integrity and core values so that where you shop, how you communicate, the work you do, and the flow of your days are all true to the light and wisdom of your soul.

Feeling joyful and creative is a subversive act when the powers running the world want you to feel anger and fear. Love, joy, bliss, and compassion are exponentially more powerful than hatred or fear due to the difference in their frequencies. Choosing to spend at least a part of your day flowing with the energy of your soul and resting in the enveloping love of your guides can be a massive contribution to a more peaceful planet, even if it's in small increments over time.

If nothing else, intend to start your day filled with peace and to move through the day as a beacon of peace, a lighthouse, an embodied star. Anchor peace in your home and garden, as you drive your car or take transit, and every time you interact with someone. Hosts of enlightened beings are ready to help you anchor that light to start changing the world.

It's going to take all of us showing up to heal the planet. Be subversively spiritual and let your love erupt exuberantly from your heart. Let it be boisterously incandescent.

In every message I've channeled, in every private session and course I do, the guides always repeat the same message: how deeply loved we are and how ready they are to help us. I hope you feel all the love that went into this book and that's flowing around you now. It's ready when you need it, and it's already with you.

FROM THE GUIDES

Archangel Michael shared some thoughts with me on the power of our resilience and the need to share our gifts in these times of chaos on the planet.

Thank you for your efforts, your perseverance, your willingness to get up again after you fall, and the resilience of your heart. It is a thing of wonder to us, for we have rested always in the comfort of the light while you have chosen to be blind to the truth of your beauty, to stumble through the mud, and to be washed anew against the rocks of these times.

Release these final bonds and chains that keep you meek and thinking small. You cannot hide your light now. You cannot convince yourself that your time to act, speak, and share is any time other than now.

Flood your surroundings with the light within you that cannot be contained. That is your path and your mission now. We love you, we hold you, we carry you, we sing to you, we remember you, we see you clearly. We are right here with you, cheering you on. What beauty be this love we have for you.

I can't wait to see what you create with this new support. Reach out and let me know.

A REVIEW REQUEST

IF YOU FIND THIS BOOK helpful, you can make a big difference.

Reviews are the most powerful way to get books out into the world, especially for self-published authors. Honest reviews help bring this book to the attention of other readers, people who might have been looking for what's shared here for a long time, or who could really use the support provided in these pages.

If you've enjoyed this book, I'd be so grateful if you could spend just five minutes leaving a review on the book's page at the retailer's website where you purchased the book. It can be as short as you like, and you can jump right to the book's review page here:

https://julesapollo.com/review/

Many thanks!

ACKNOWLEDGMENTS

THIS BOOK GESTATED FOR MANY years before I wrote it because I didn't feel like I had anything worthwhile to share and I didn't know how to explain what I did in such a way that people would understand how it could help them. It feels so great to finally complete it!

AJ Harper and Laura Stone of Top Three Book Workshop taught me how to approach and outline this book so it just flowed out with creative joy. It felt magical. And I'm grateful to the Top Three Book Workshop writing community for companionship, support, and inspiration. Zoë Bird not only did a great job copyediting the book; her kind support and gentle suggestions also helped me enjoy the process when I had feared it. KellyAnn Bessa kicked it with her proofreading, finishing well ahead of schedule. I was told Choi Messer would bring me a beautifully typeset book, she exceeded my high expectations.

Some key people helped me work through the internal stuff holding me back from sharing this material. I'm indebted to Tara Mohr, Marie Forleo, Jeannette Maw, Denise Duffield Thomas, Joanna Penn, and Sonia Choquette for their programs, teaching and compassionate wisdom. I've returned to their words and programs many times over the years. Sonia has been my biggest spiritual influence. Her down-to-earth approach of sharing details about her work with her guides gave me a reference point to return to as I tried to find my own voice and confidence in my work.

When I was stuck in old worries while writing, I turned to Michelle Lowbridge's gentle, profound energy work and the unshakable positive thinking of Jeannette Maw to free me.

My early readers had great suggestions that strengthened the book: many thanks to Dr. Kerry Burnight, Marcia Dawood, Kristi Murdock, Kate Lynde, Vickie Lanthier, Sandra Furber, Carole Mitchell, Annie Sterling, Marian Dolan, Julie Jaycox and Mara Yale.

I'm grateful to my spiritual support team for always helping me and making our work together a great adventure. I drew inspiration for productive creativity from the lives and works of Jane Austen, Louisa May Alcott, and Beryl Markham. Huzzah to their memories and trailblazing work.

I'm grateful to my students, clients, listeners, and readers who encouraged me to keep sharing.

As always, the biggest blessings in my life are my three sons. I'm so lucky to be their mom and so proud to see what wise, caring, and compassionate men they've become.